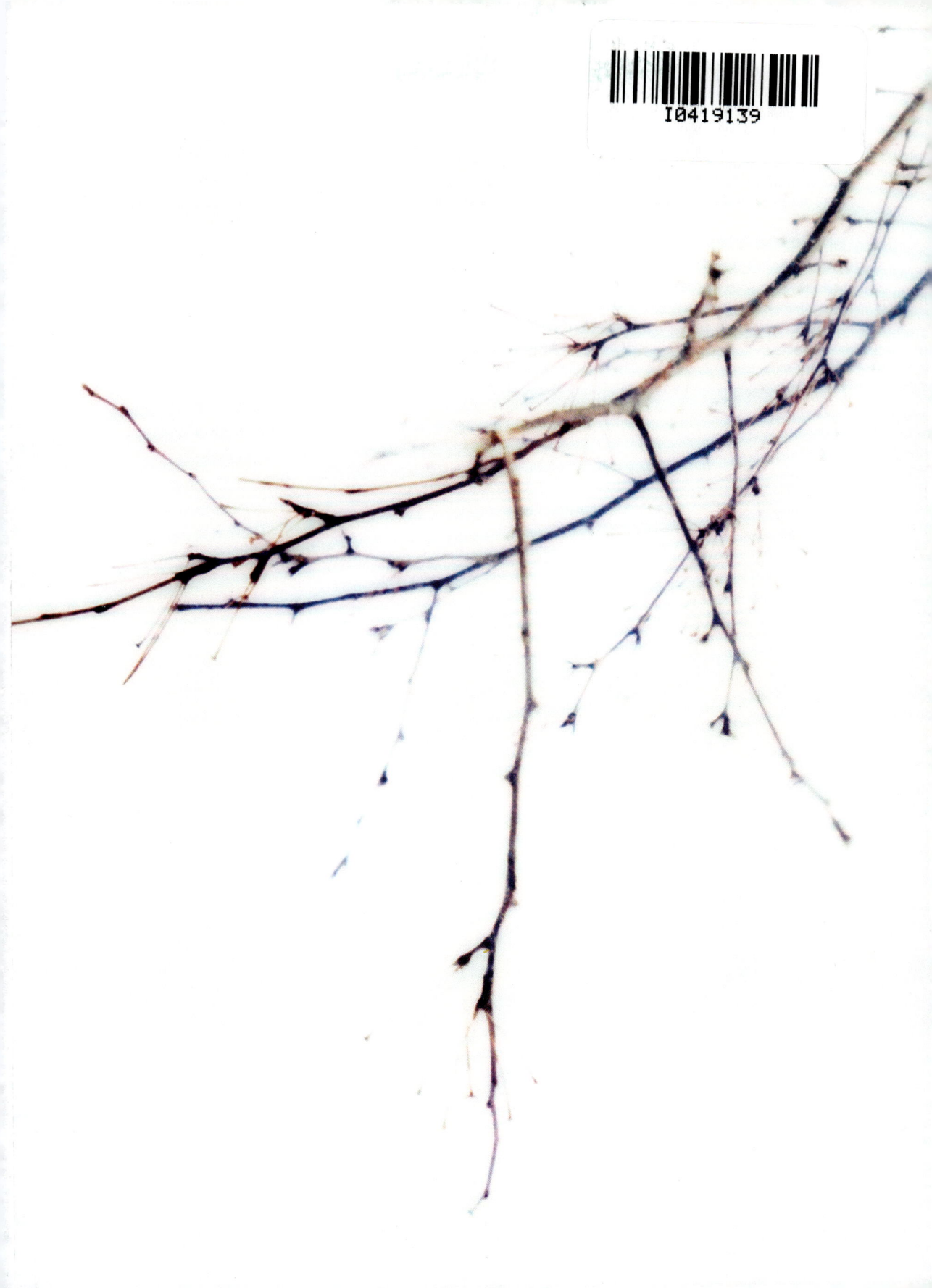

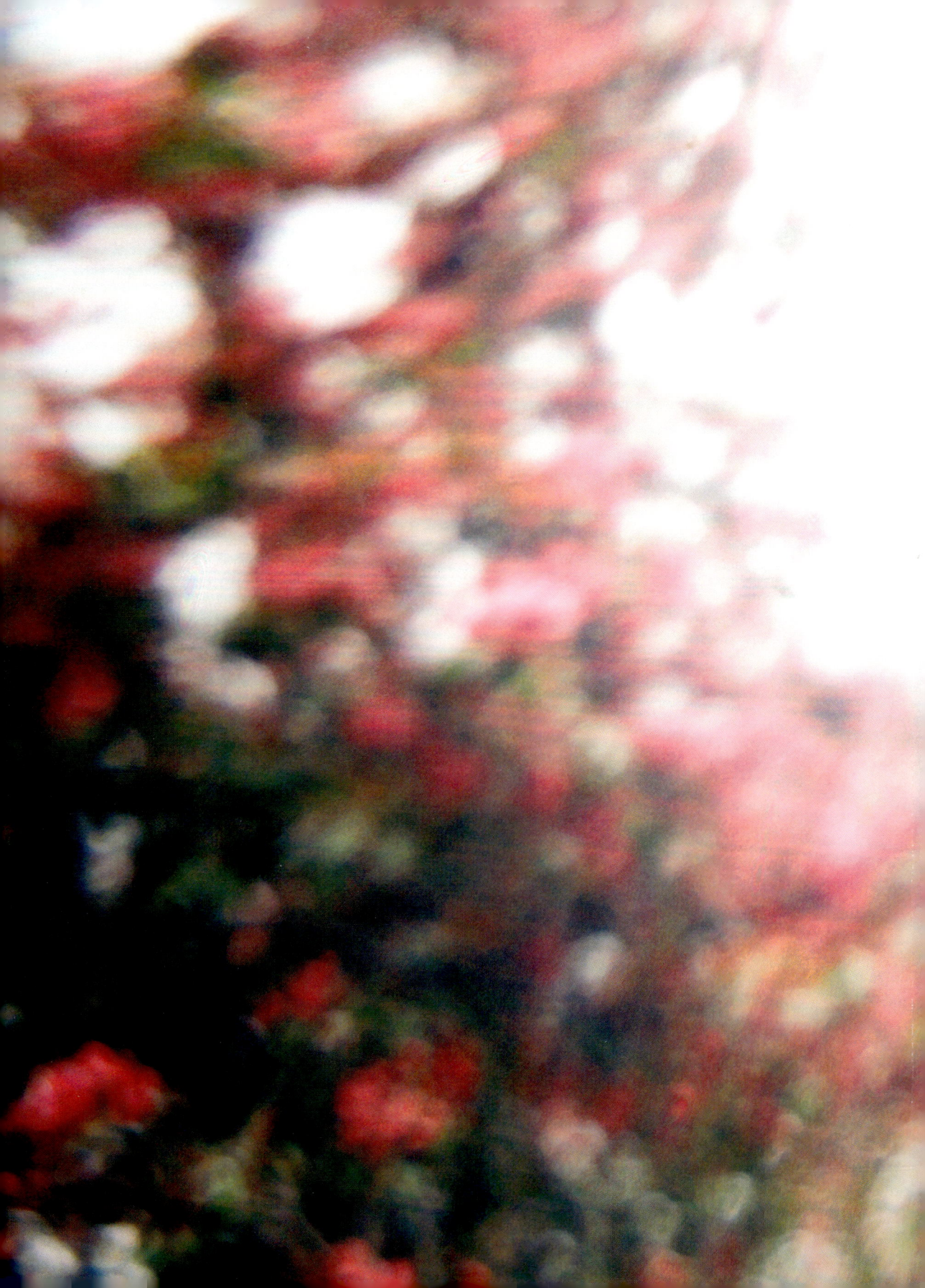

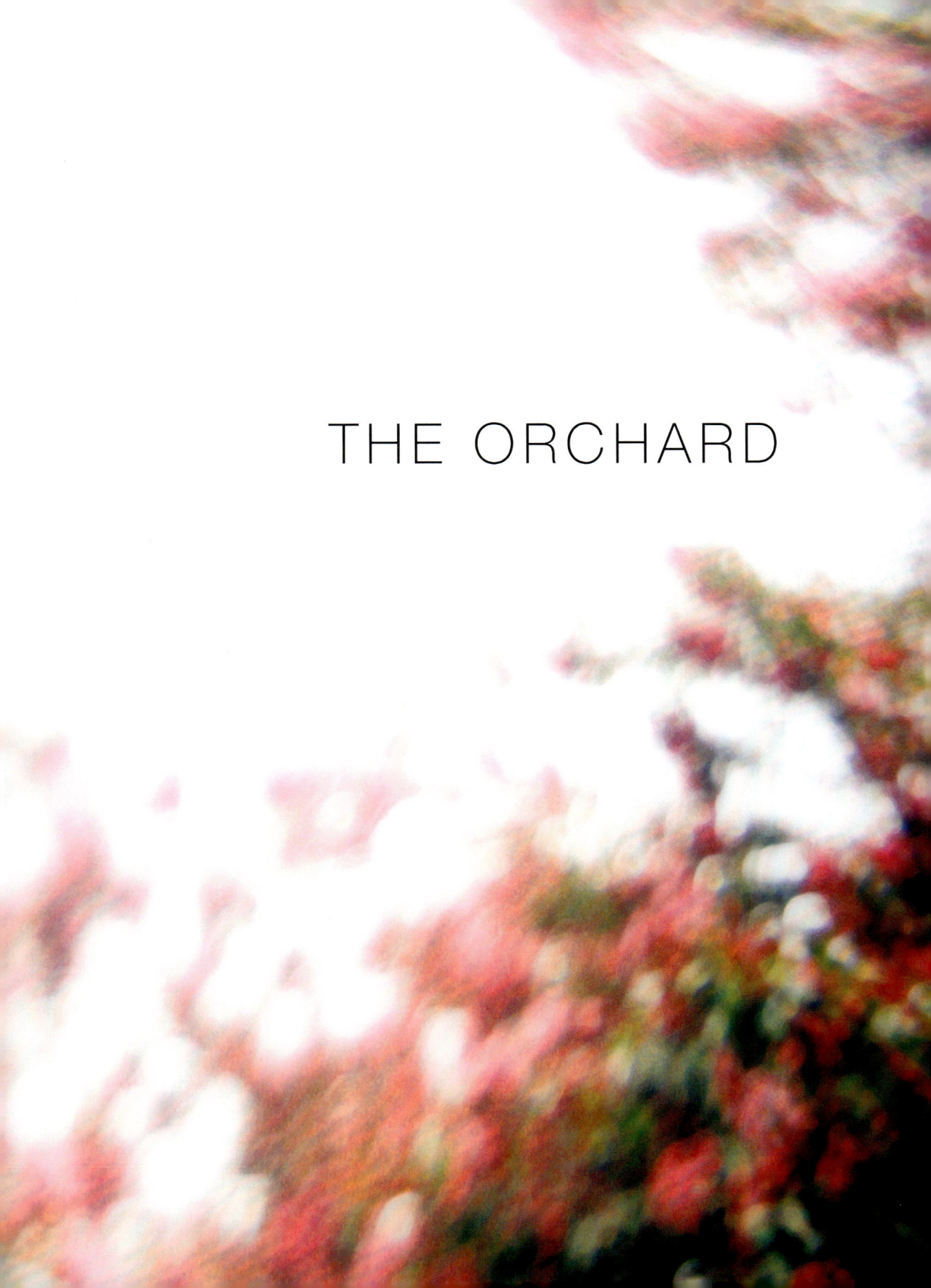

THE ORCHARD

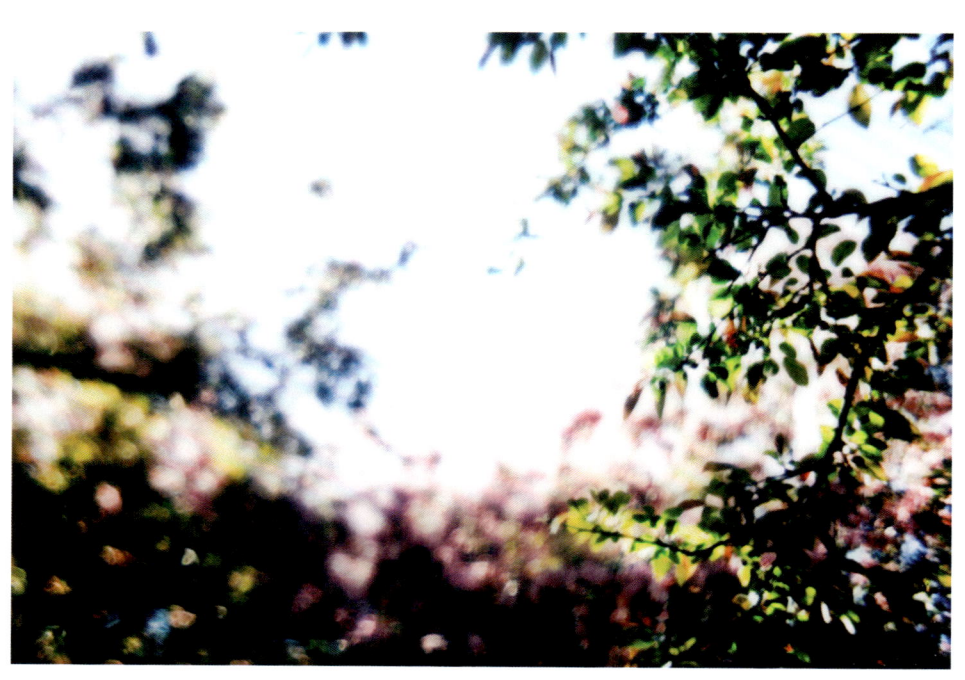

THE ORCHARD

SUSAN WEISS

Introduction by Eve O. Schaub

GREEN WRITERS PRESS | *Brattleboro, Vermont*

PRINTED IN THE UNITED STATES

10 9 8 7 6 5 4 3 2 1

GREEN WRITERS PRESS IS A VERMONT-BASED PUBLISHER WHOSE MISSION IS TO SPREAD A MESSAGE OF HOPE AND RENEWAL THROUGH THE WORDS AND IMAGES WE PUBLISH. THROUGHOUT WE WILL ADHERE TO OUR COMMITMENT TO PRESERVING AND PROTECTING THE NATURAL RESOURCES OF THE EARTH. TO THAT END, A PERCENTAGE OF OUR PROCEEDS WILL BE DONATED TO ENVIRONMENTAL ACTIVIST GROUPS. GREEN WRITERS PRESS GRATEFULLY ACKNOWLEDGES SUPPORT FROM INDIVIDUAL DONORS, FRIENDS, AND READERS TO HELP SUPPORT THE ENVIRONMENT AND OUR PUBLISHING INITIATIVE.

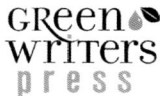

Giving Voice to Writers & Artists
Who will Make the World a Better Place

GREEN WRITERS PRESS | BRATTLEBORO, VERMONT
WWW.GREENWRITERSPRESS.COM

ISBN: 979-8-9883820-8-9

PRINTED BY PURITAN PRESS, HOLLIS, NEW HAMPSHIRE, ON 30% POST-CONSUMER FIBER WITH STOCK SHEETS THAT ARE FOREST STEWARDSHIP COUNCIL® (FSC®) CERTIFIED THAT COME FROM MANAGED FORESTS THAT GUARANTEE RESPONSIBLE ENVIRONMENTAL, SOCIAL, AND ECONOMIC PRACTICES.

INTRODUCTION

What does a tree know about a pandemic?

EVE O. SCHAUB

Humans take great comfort in trees. It makes me wonder if they take comfort in us. If we all went away, would the trees miss us? I have heard that trees communicate with one another along the vast network of roots under the earth, like an invisible web. Separate, solitary, but fundamentally connected.

What does a tree know about a pandemic?

During times of crisis, one looks for sources of beauty in the world. An orchard of ornamental trees is a thing of striking beauty all unto itself: a world within a world. Its scale is comfortable: people sized. Like a low-canopied forest, the trees provide shade in summer and stand sentinel in winter. Fall presents an opera of wind and leaves, and spring is ever drinking its coffee: anxious to arrive and anxious to leave.

In the orchard, sweeping themes of color emerge and recede in tsunami waves. Icy blues and whites give way to fantastical pinks and savage greens, folding over at last to bawdy oranges and browns. A unified body composed of harmonious parts, the orchard turns easily—like a flock of geese—and begins again.

Rooted as they are, do trees have choices? What about personalities? Or opinions? Would we feel differently about them if we gave each one a name and could say, "Jennifer is in bloom today" or "Samuel lost a branch in the storm"? It isn't too hard to imagine, is it, that they might feel warmly towards us when we sat in their shadow after raking their leaves into a pile . . . or that they could be fascinated by the nest of sticks that appears in their branches one spring?

The imagery and palette of the orchard evoke for the viewer concentrated meditations on the natural cycle: life, death, and rebirth, and the associated emotions of joy, grief, and hope. Even in the grips of a deathly winter, there appears a path in the snow signifying the continuation of life. Trees at night appear as cloud-like apparitions from a dream. A solitary trunk stands like a headstone. Riots of color-pinpoints cluster like fireworks in one moment, while in another they soften shyly into powder puffs. Abstracted branches slice through mottled skies.

Trees have few aspirations, and it might be best that way. They have no need to travel to Sweden or visit the Grand Canyon. They will never write the great American novel or discover a cure for disease. They exist to be what they are, and they are supremely good at it, most of the time. A tree, even a small, ornamental crab apple, knows nothing about a pandemic and yet everything about what it needs to know: it grows. It talks, perhaps, to its neighbors about the chipmunks and the beetles. Maybe it even senses us when we are there, and when we are not.

It knows things. It feels the raindrops and waits for spring.

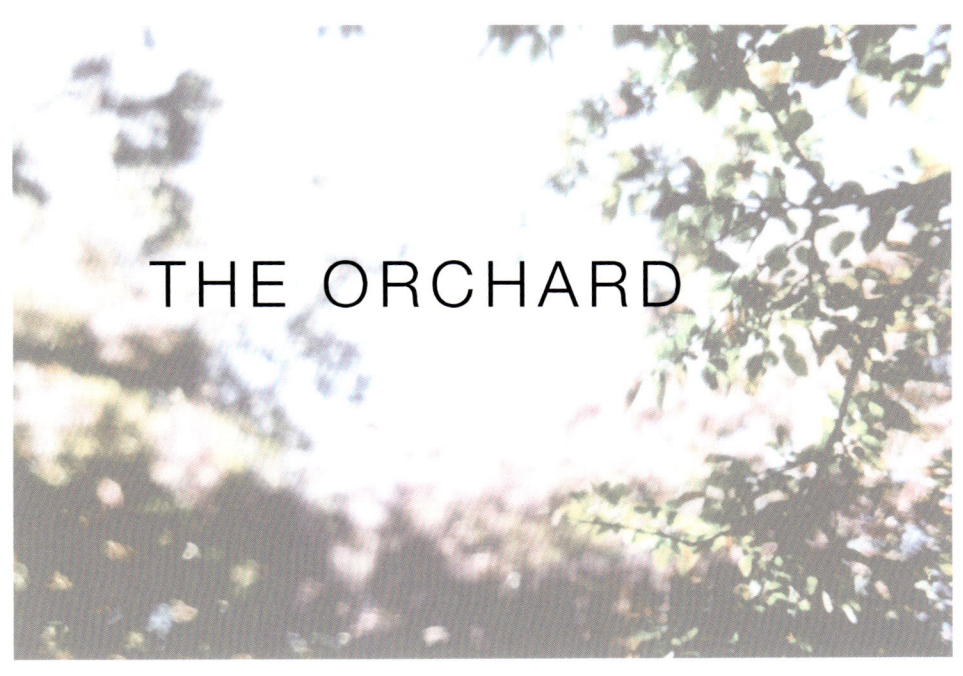

THE ORCHARD

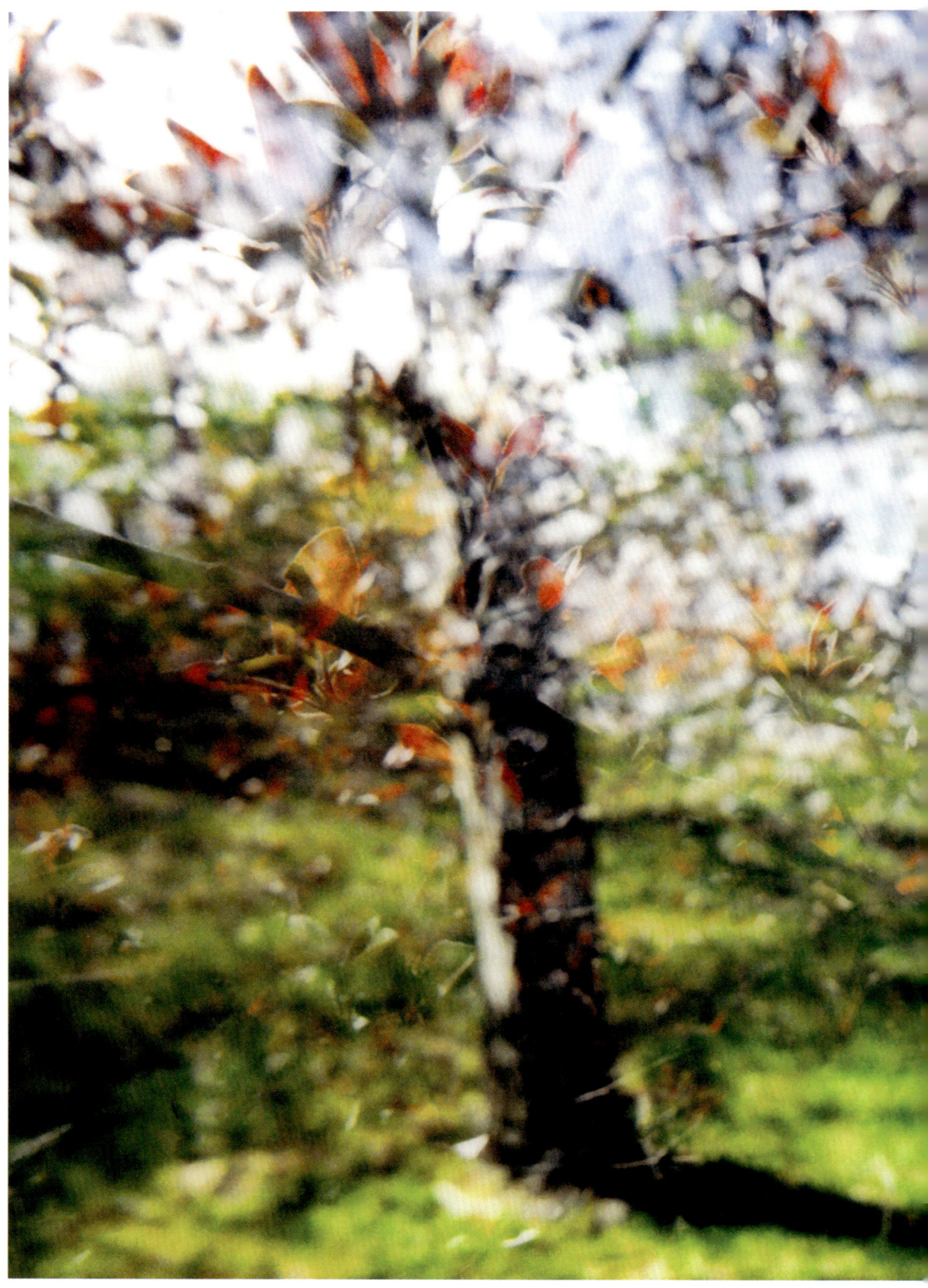

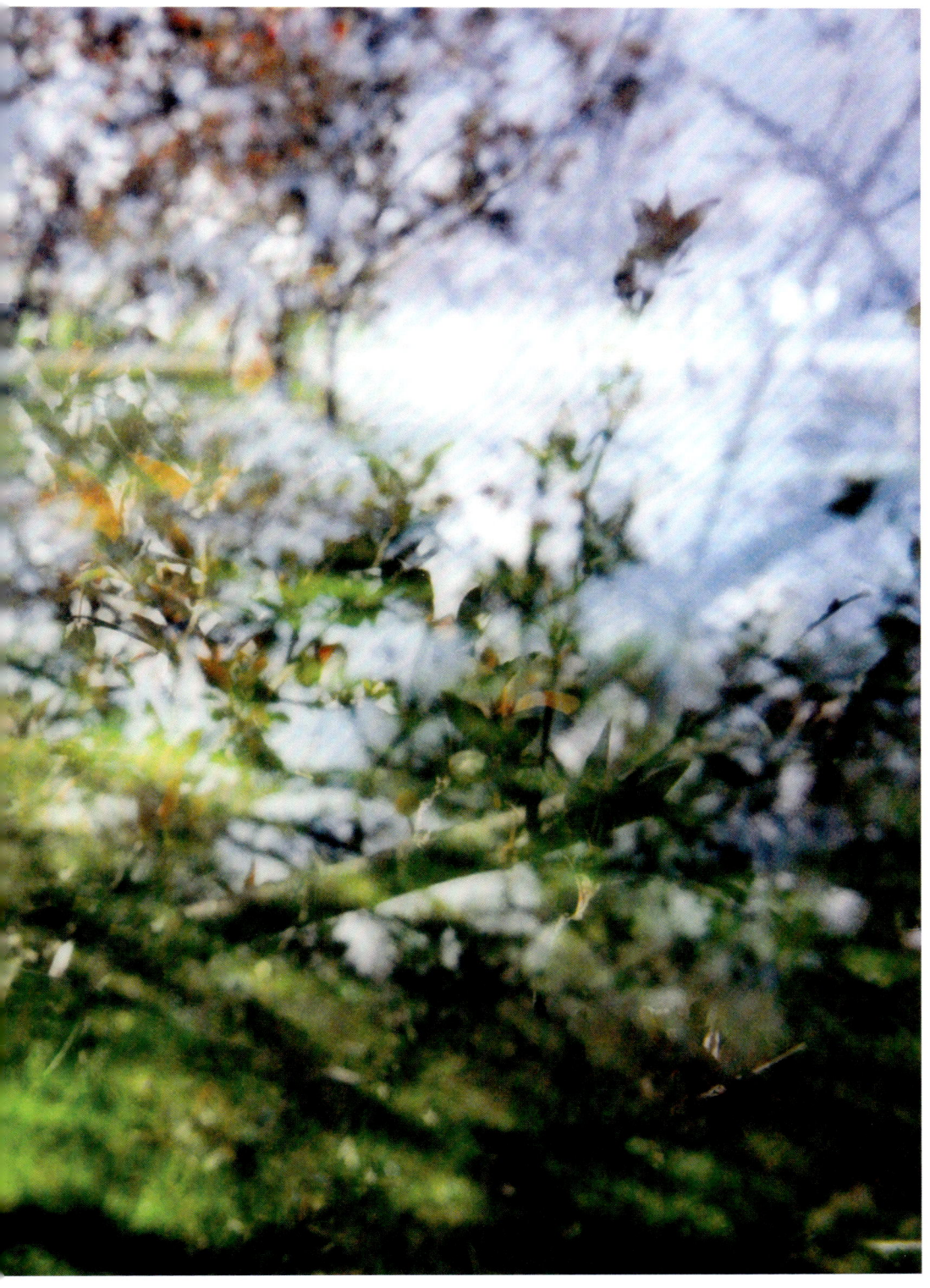

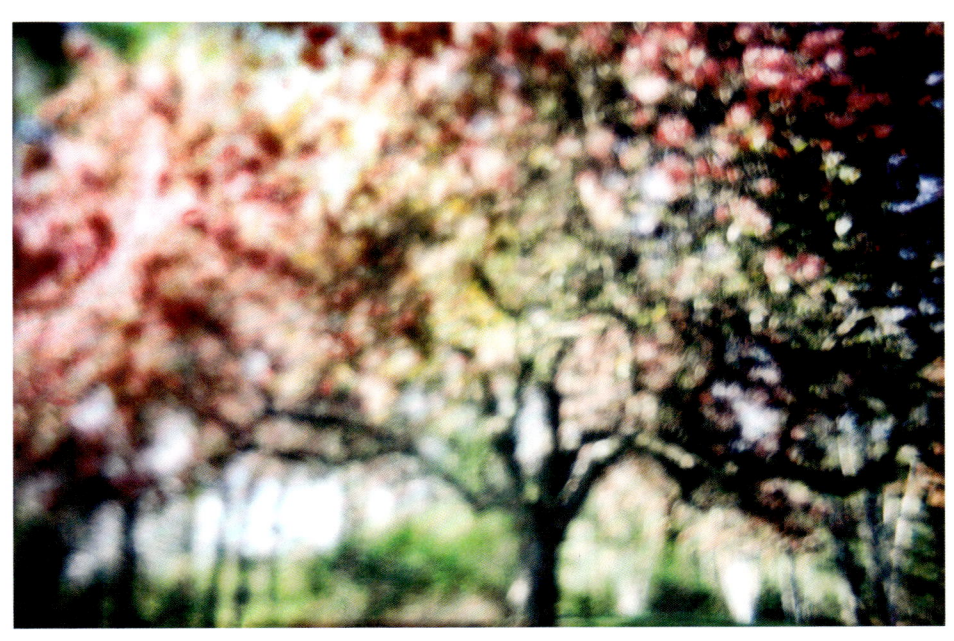

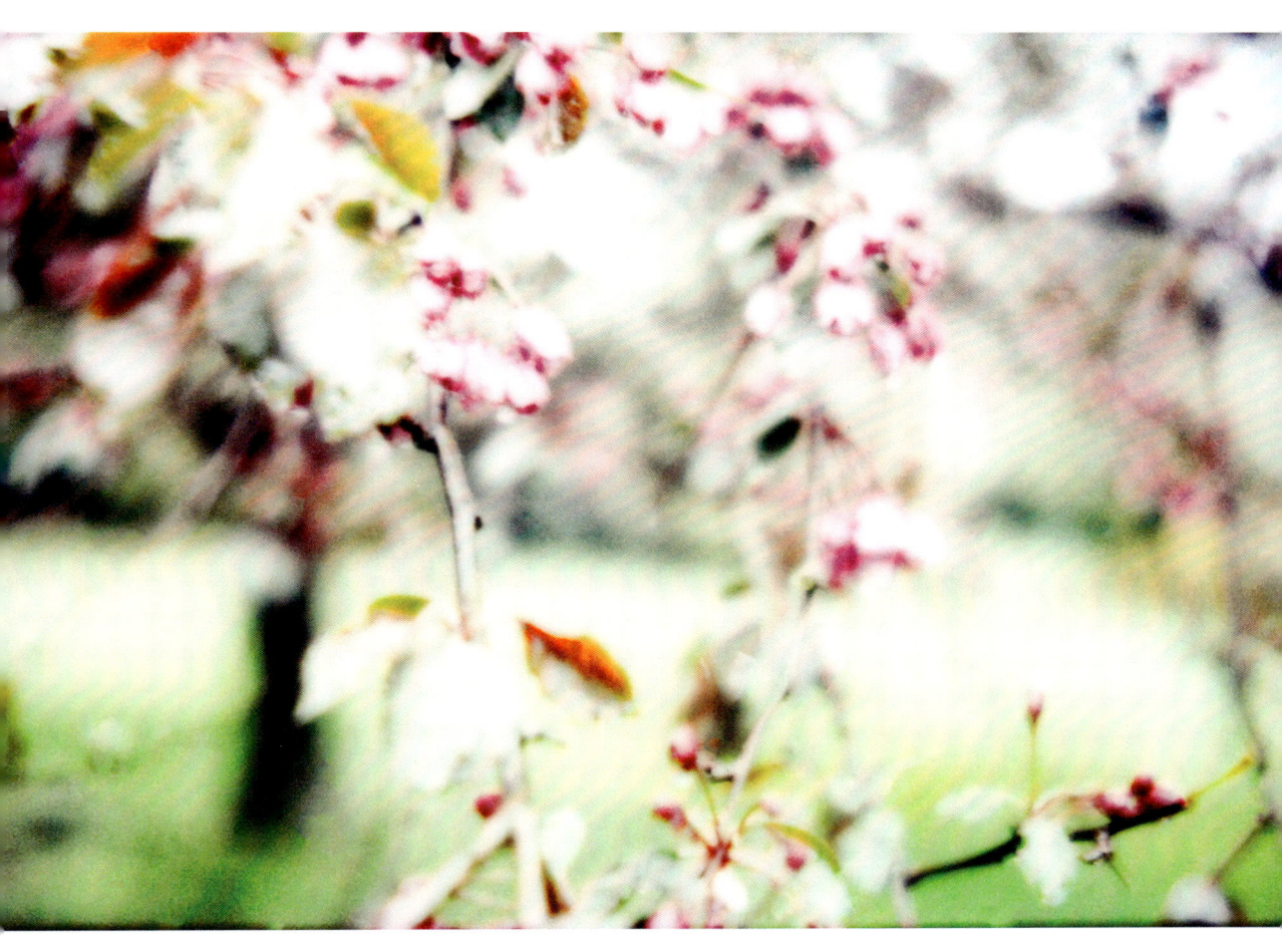

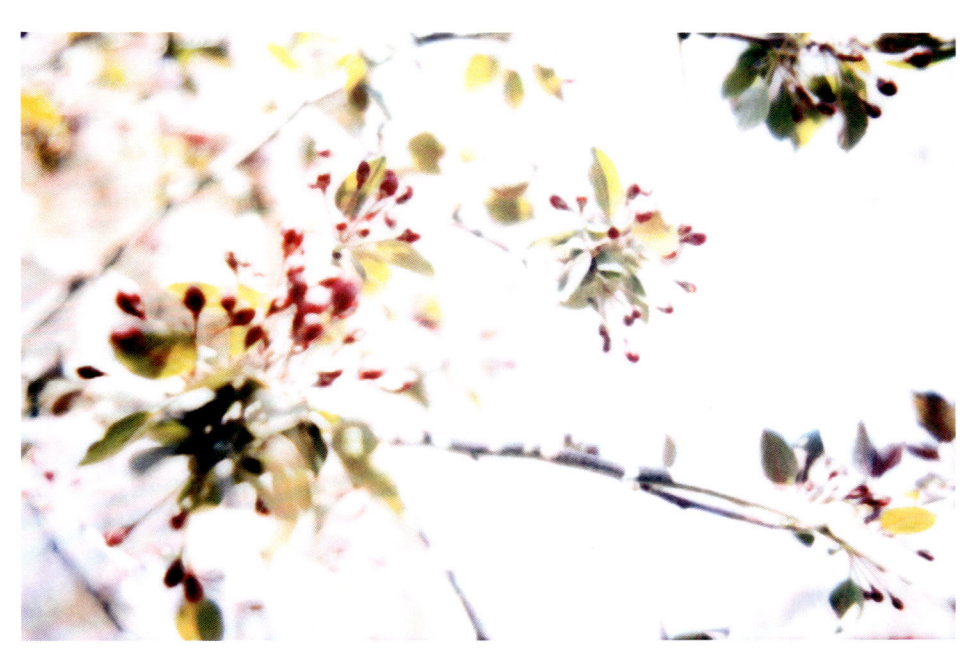

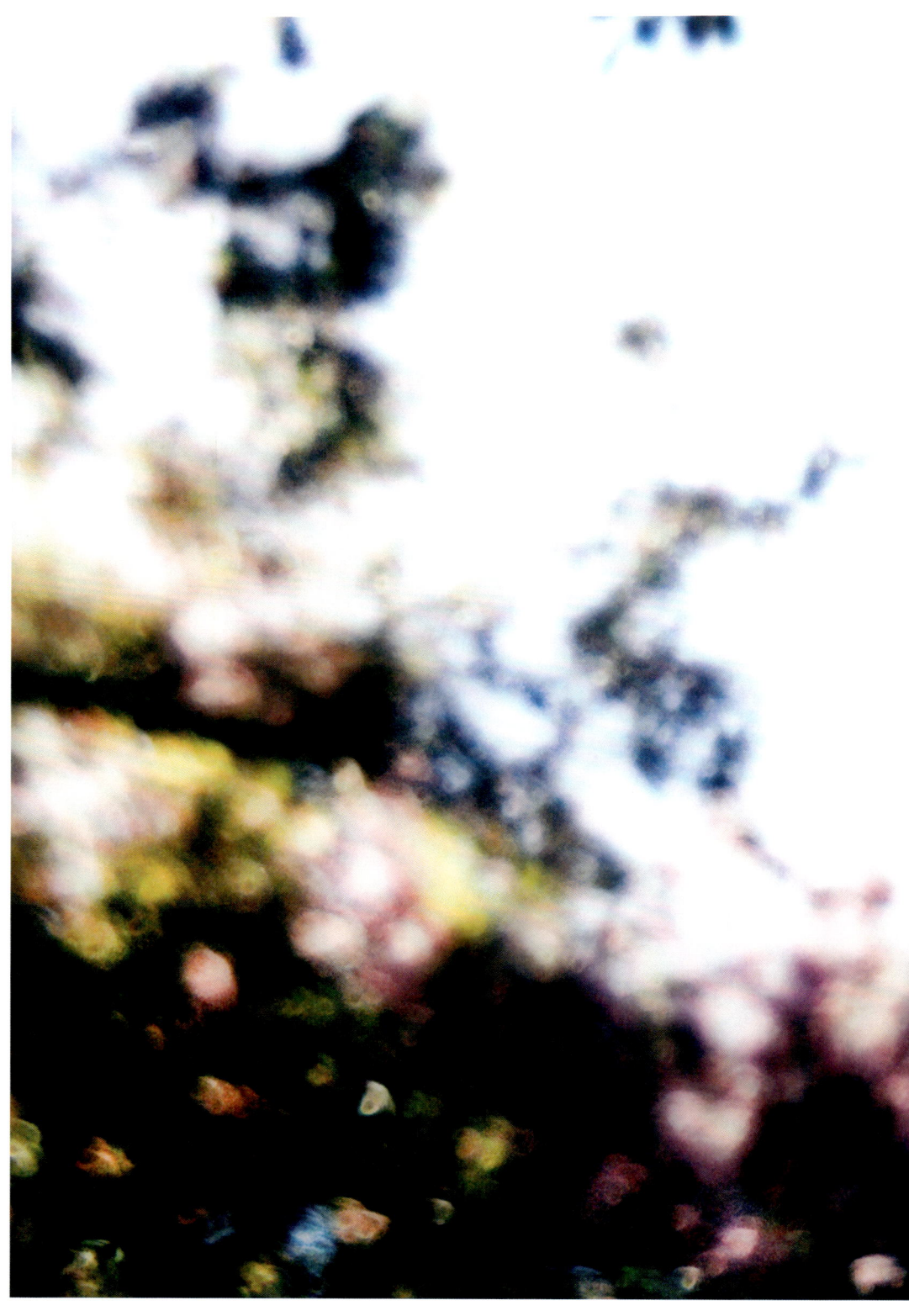

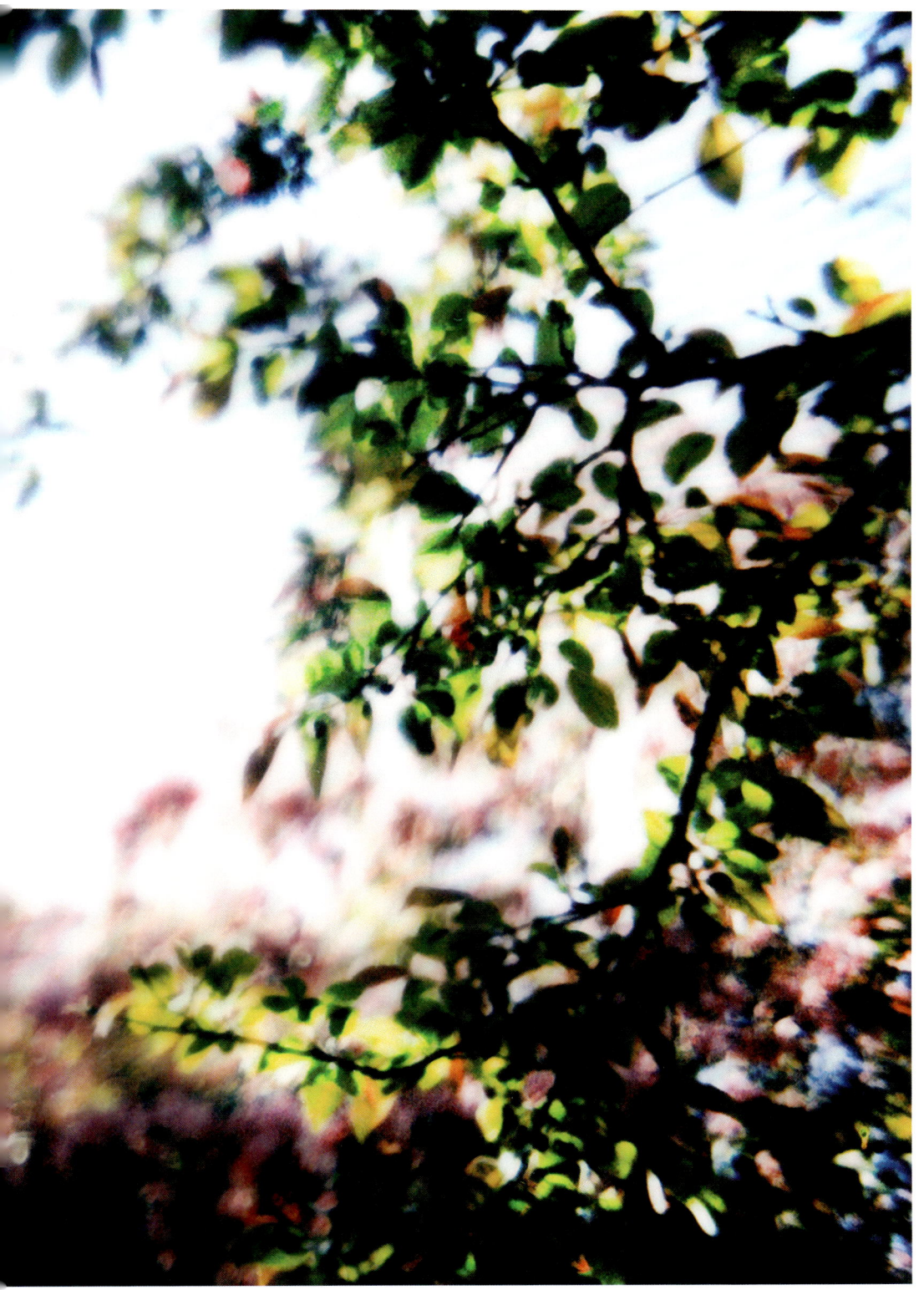

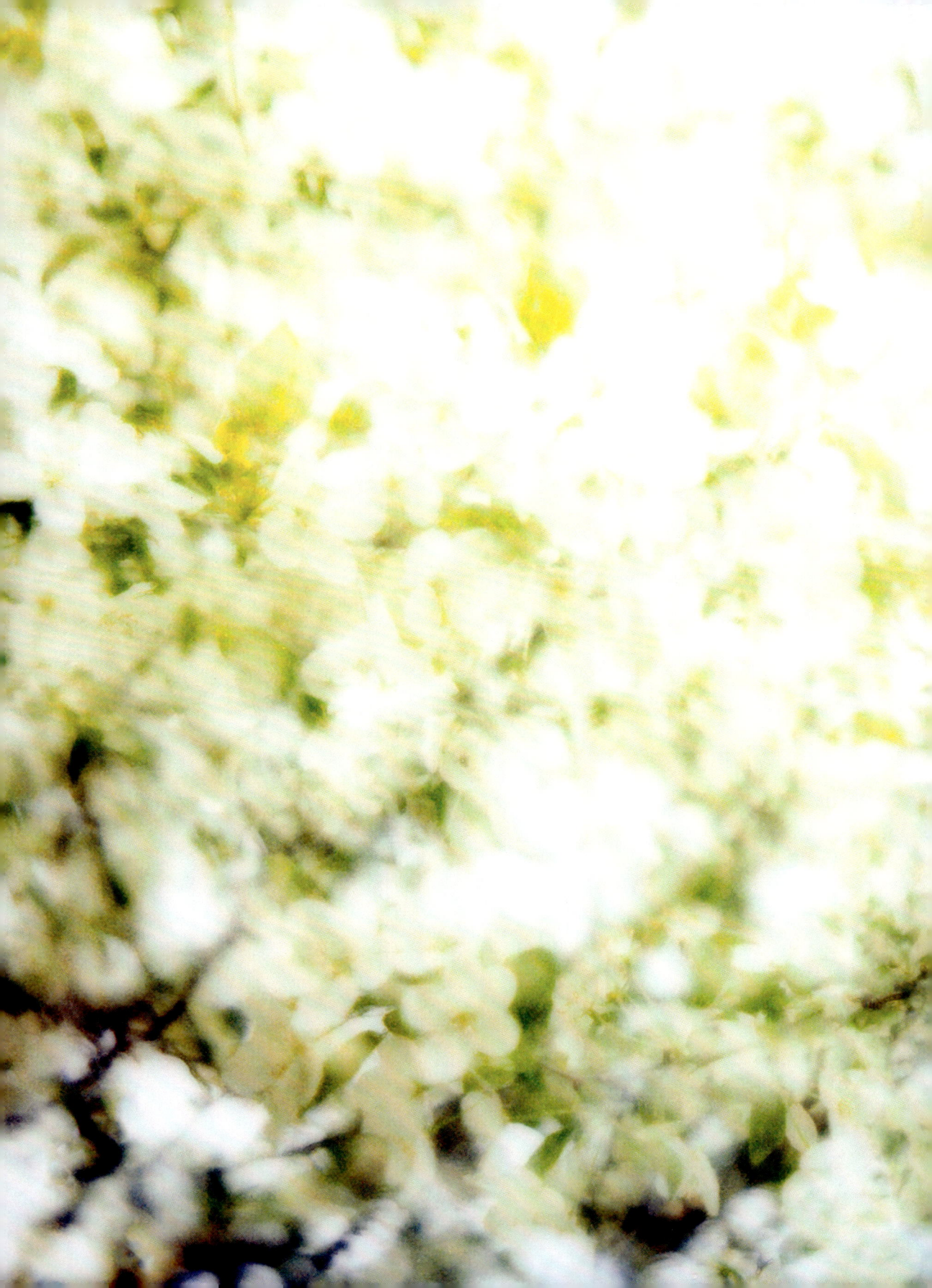

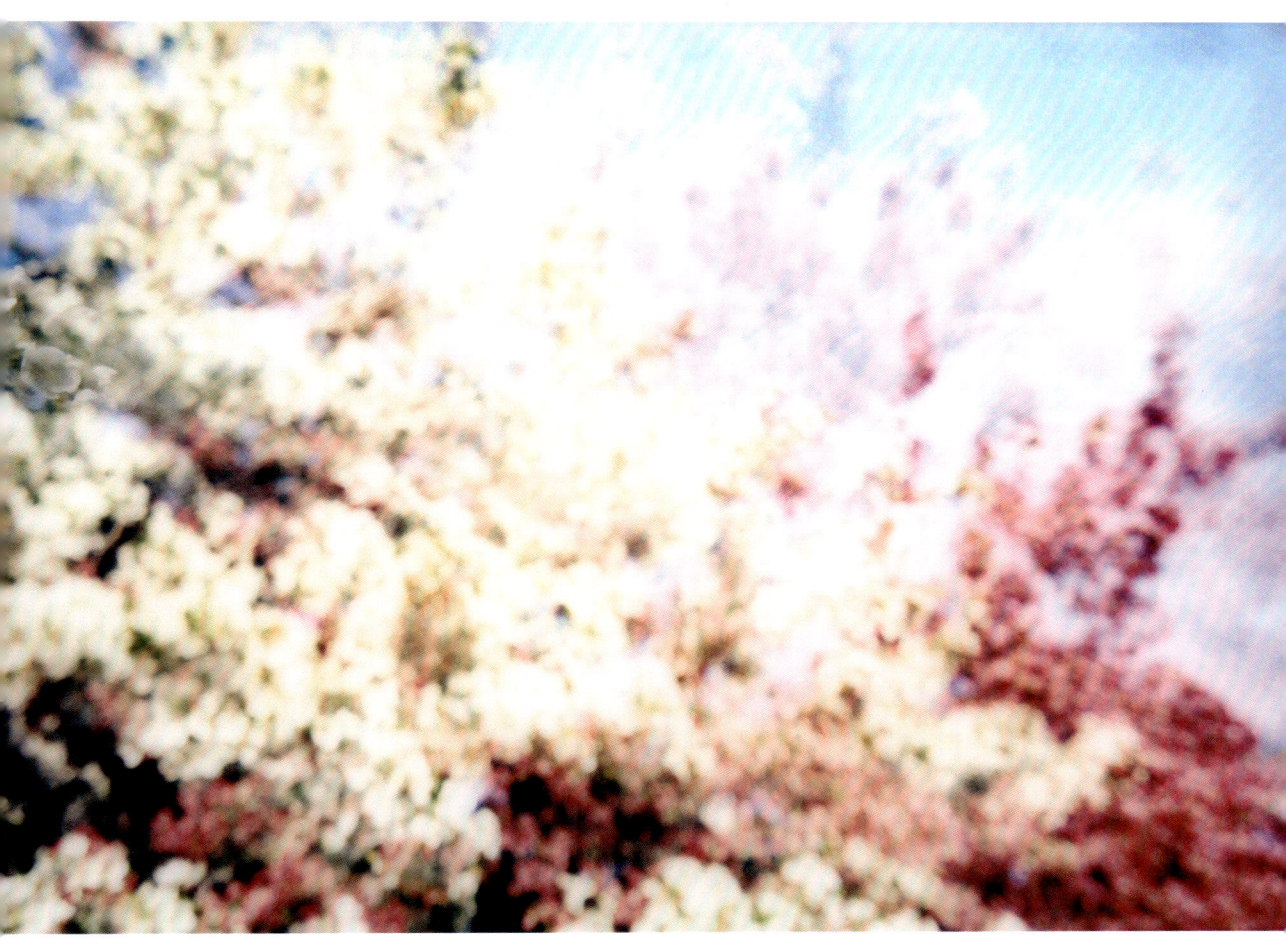

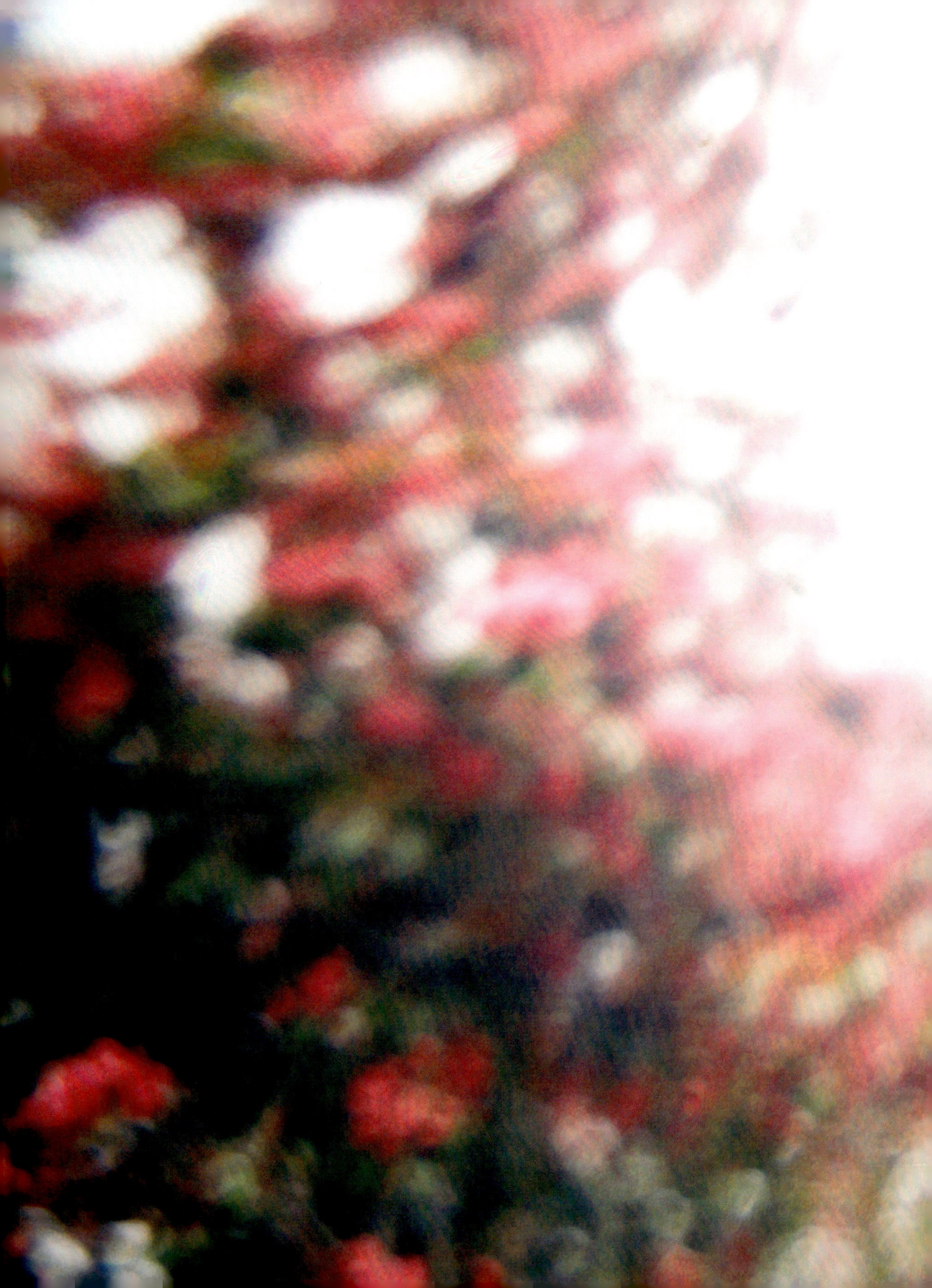

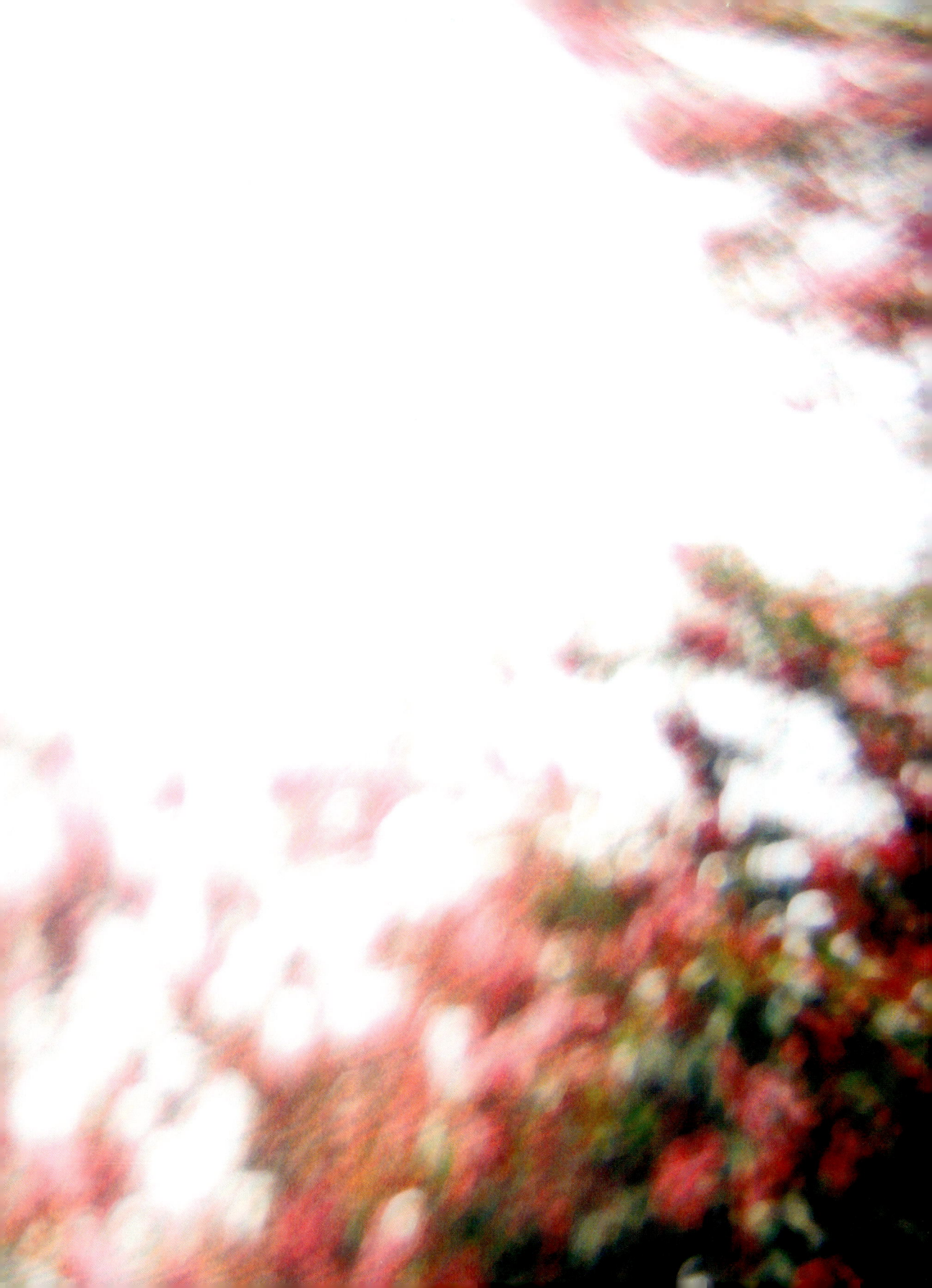

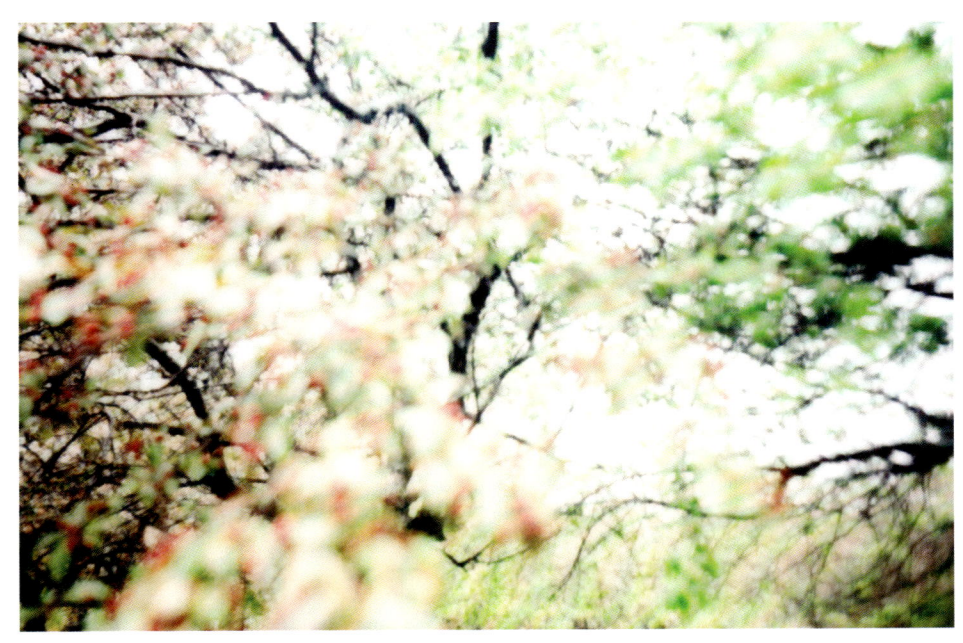

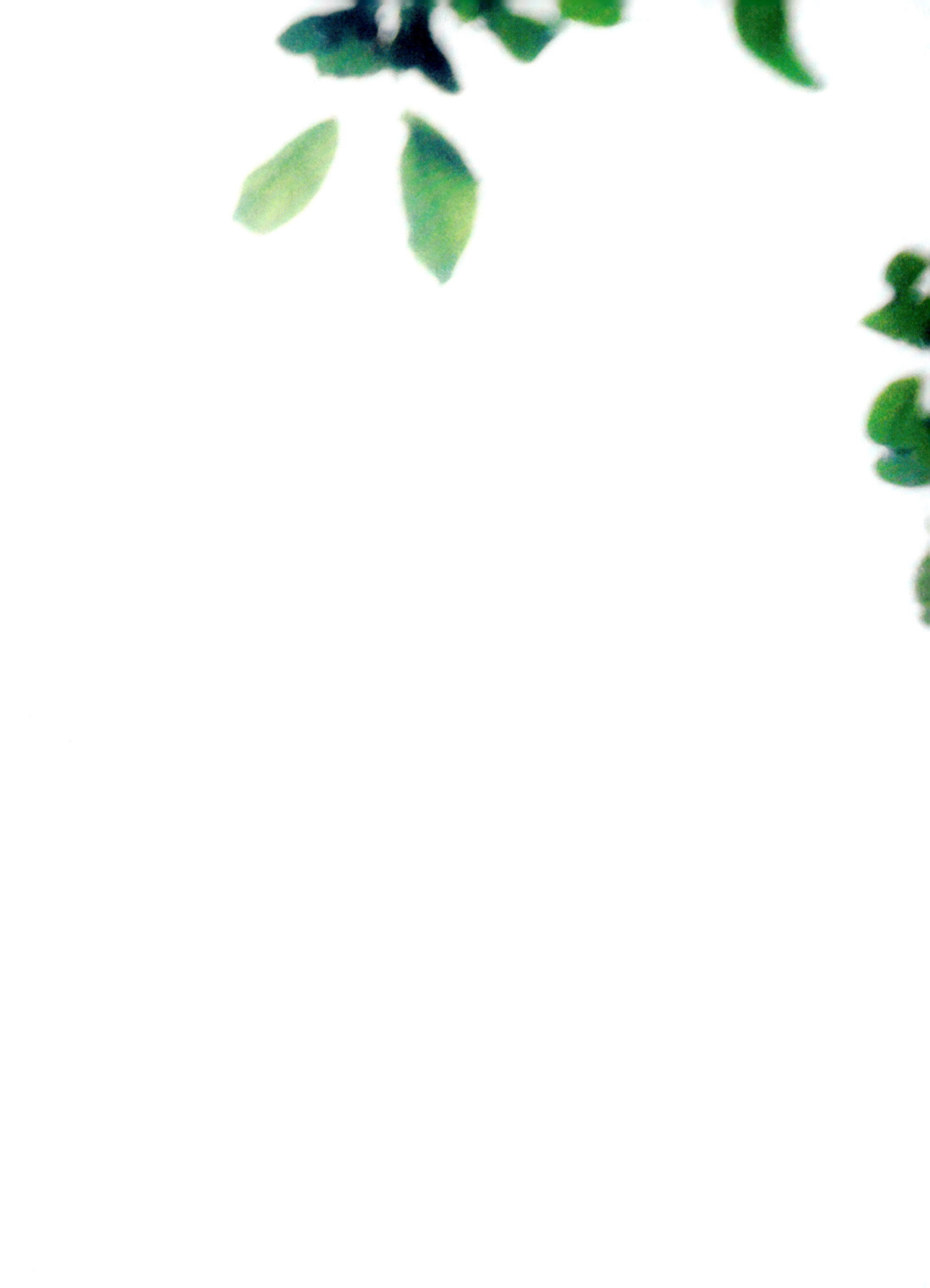

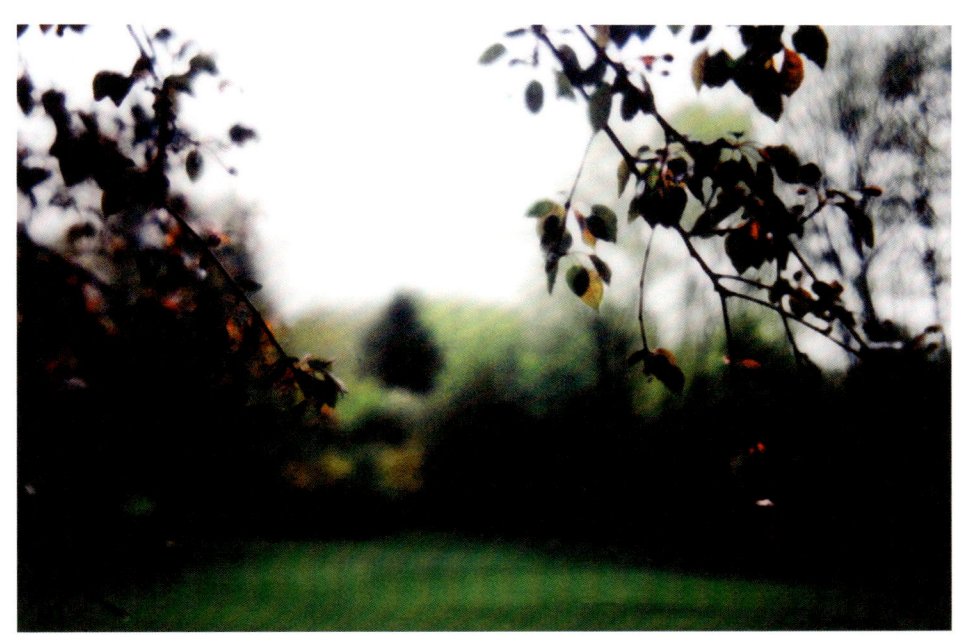

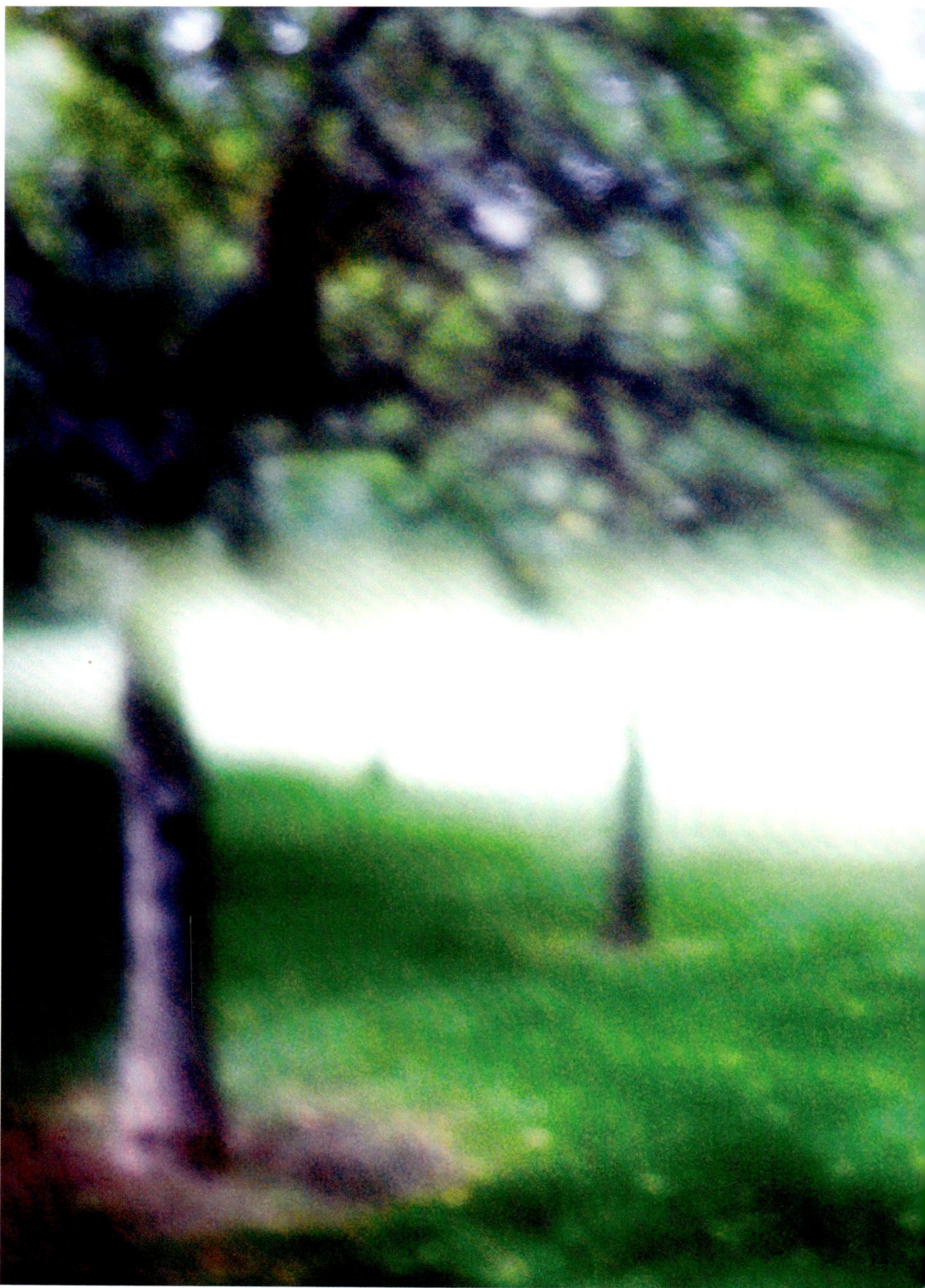

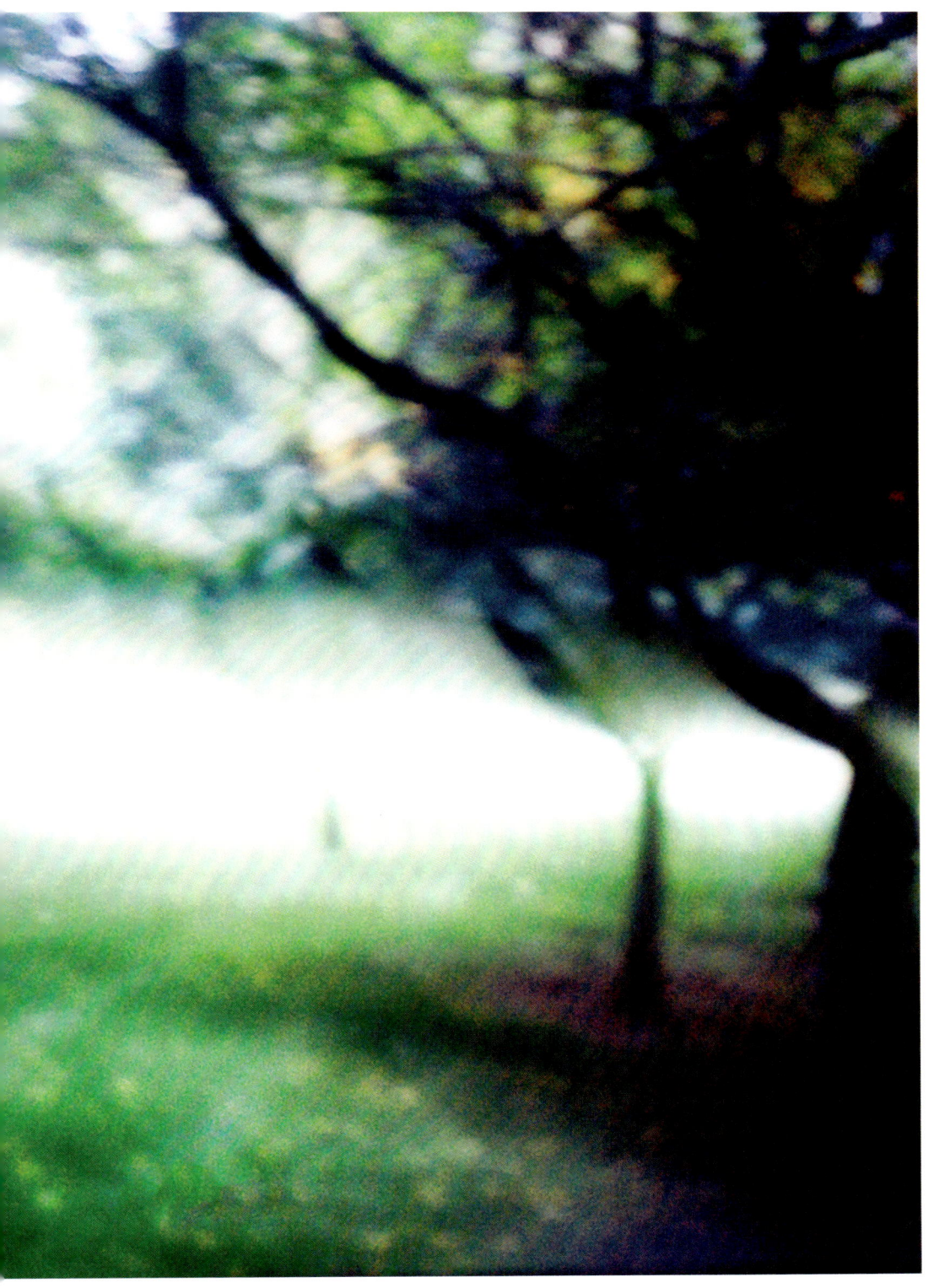

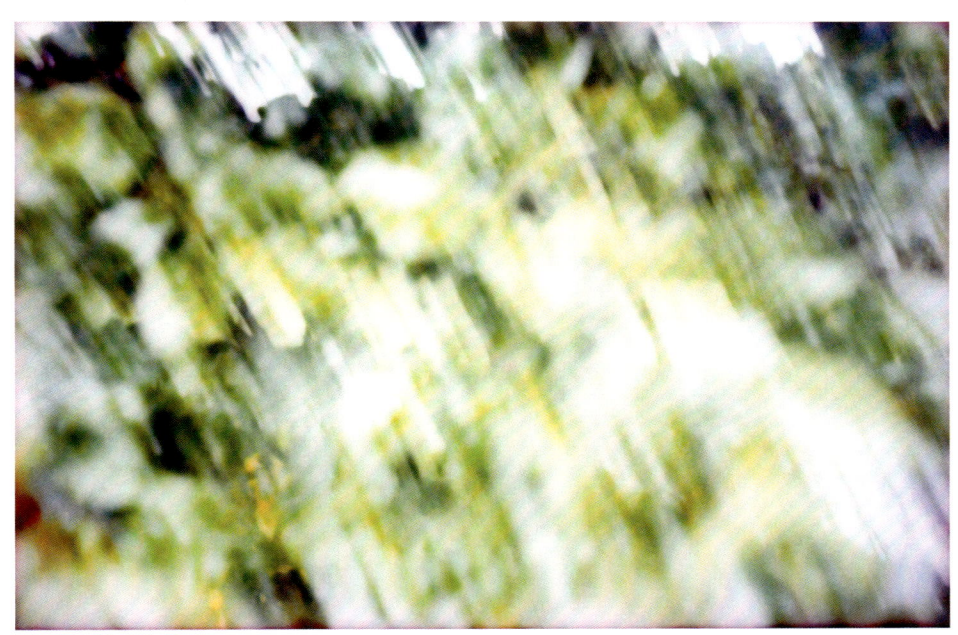

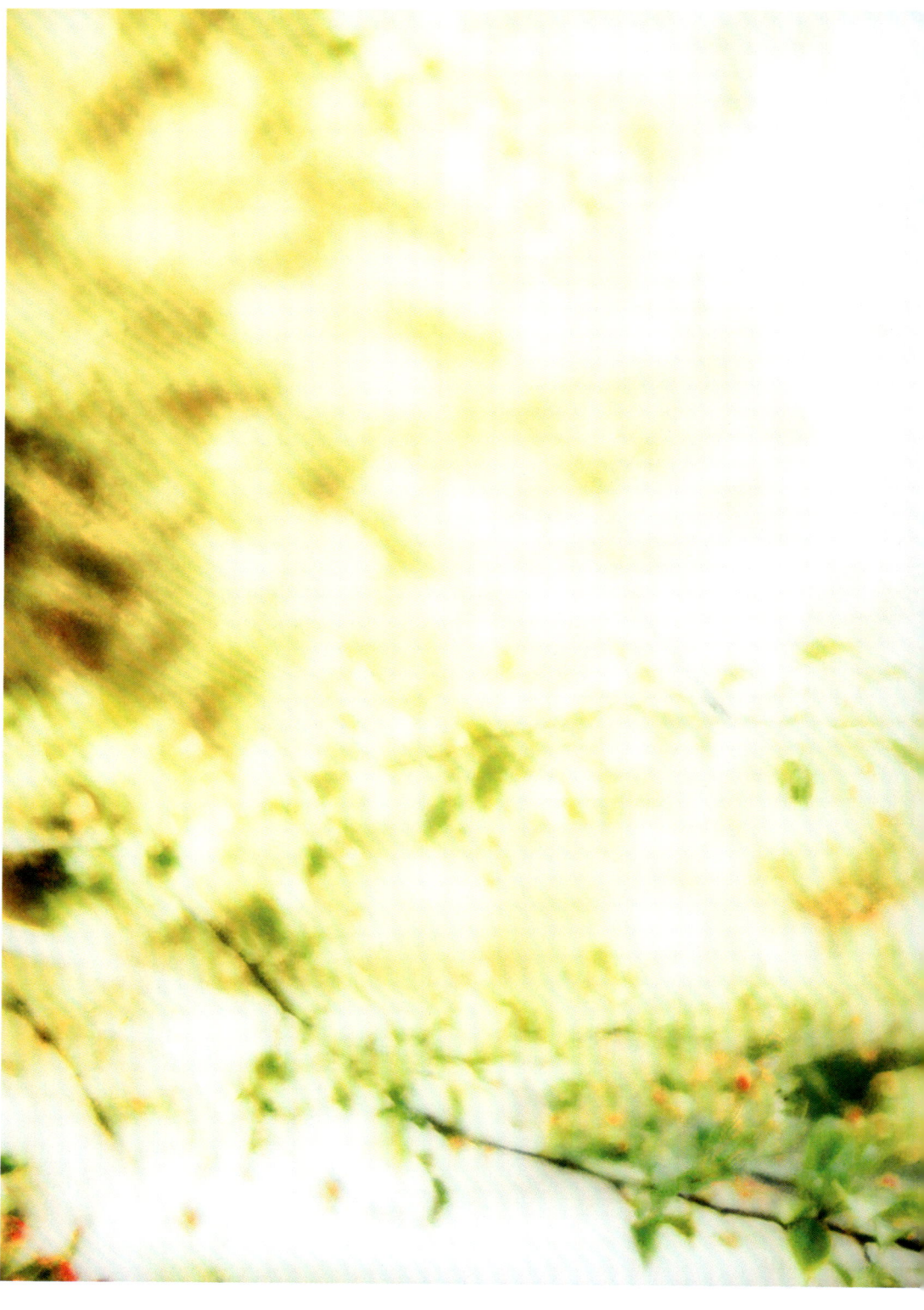

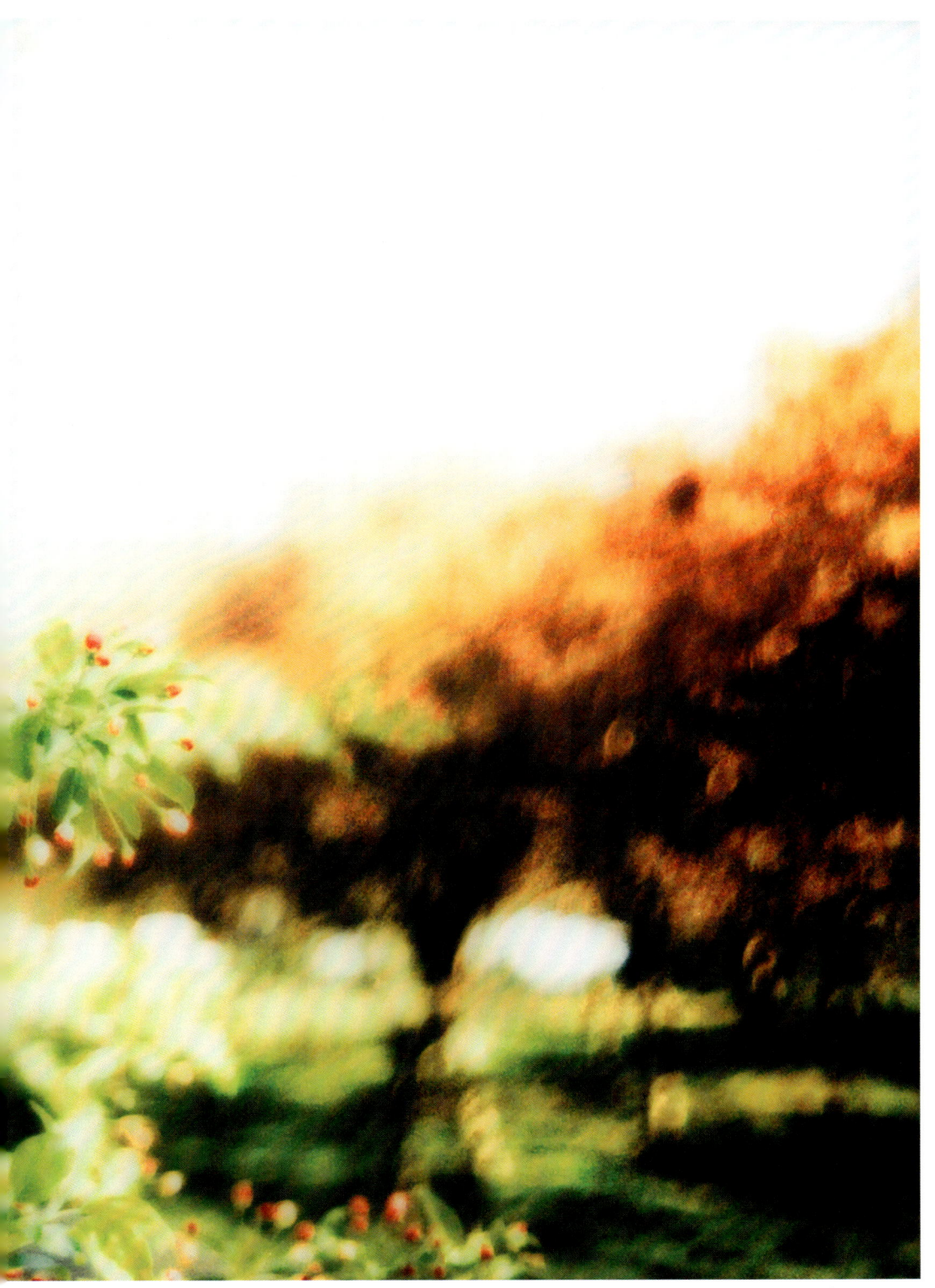

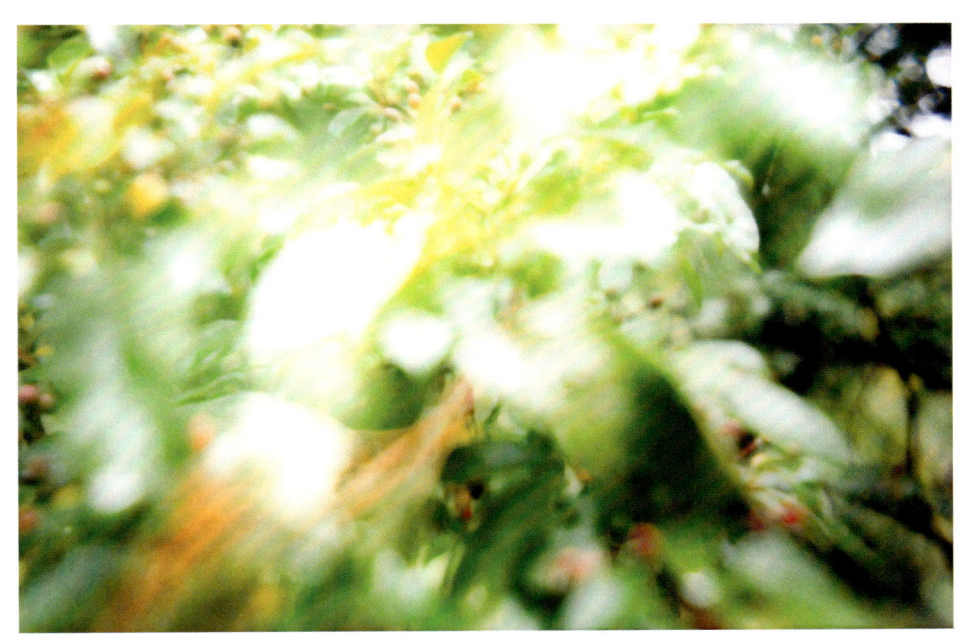

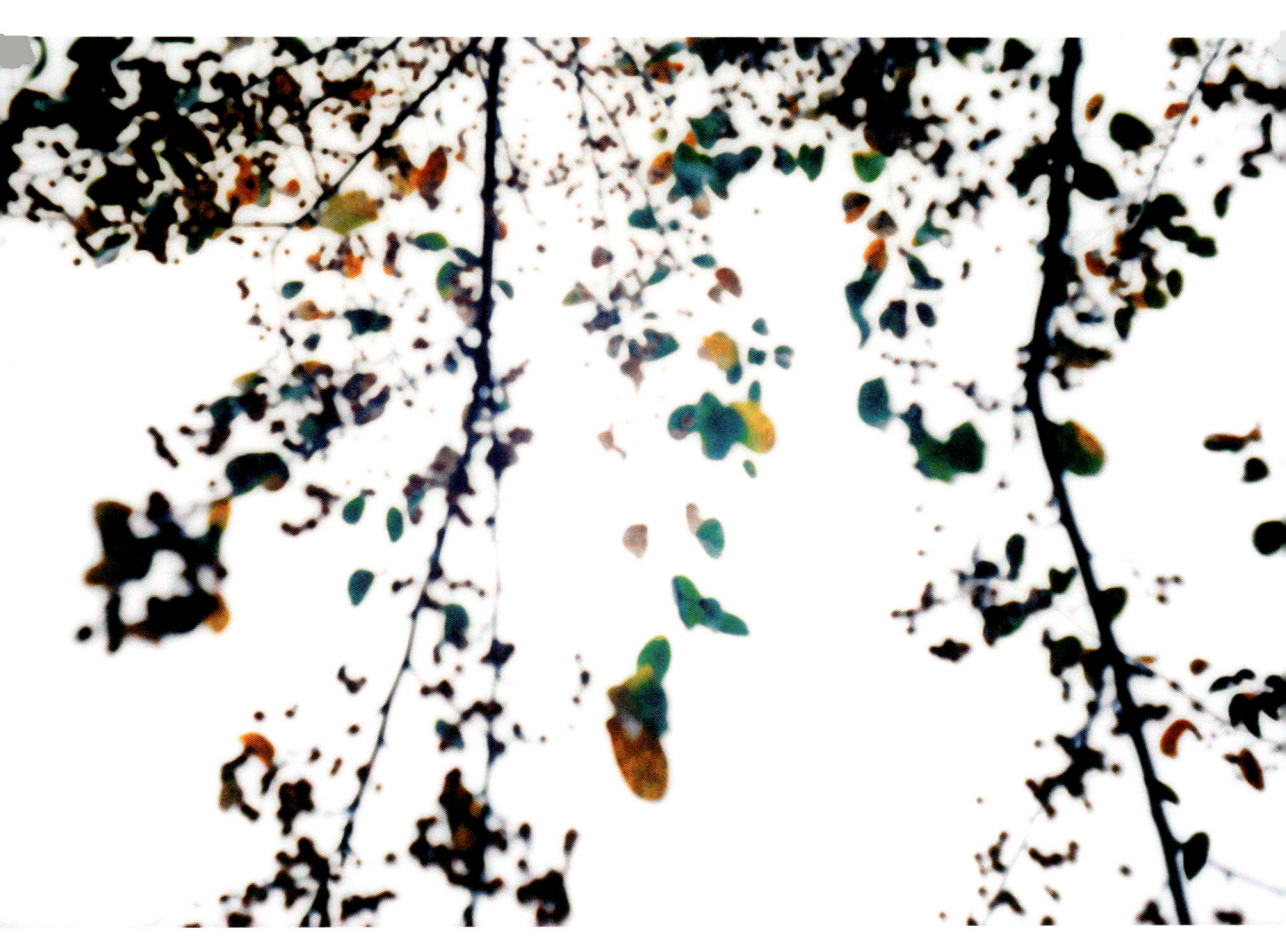

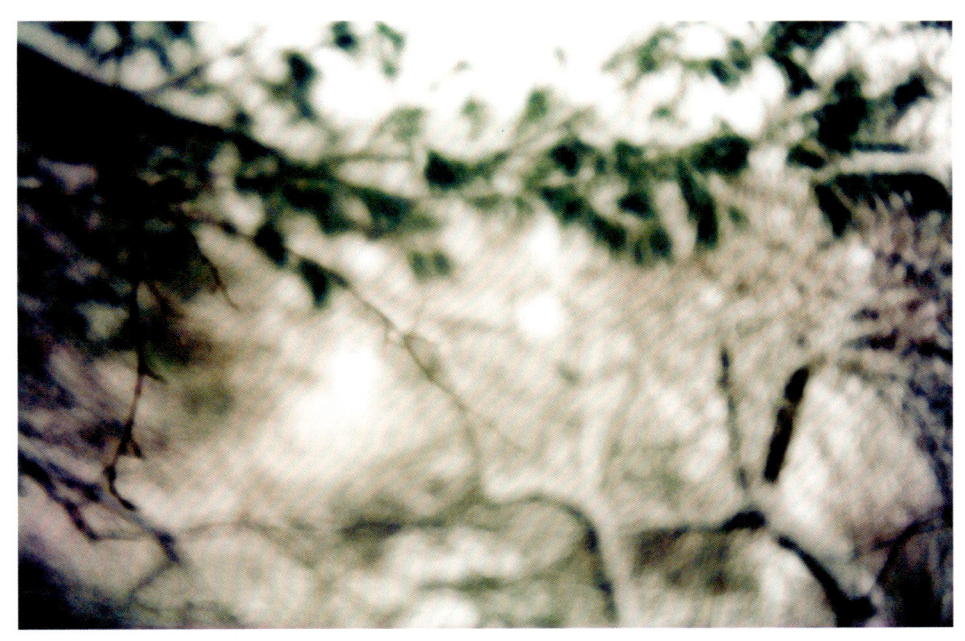

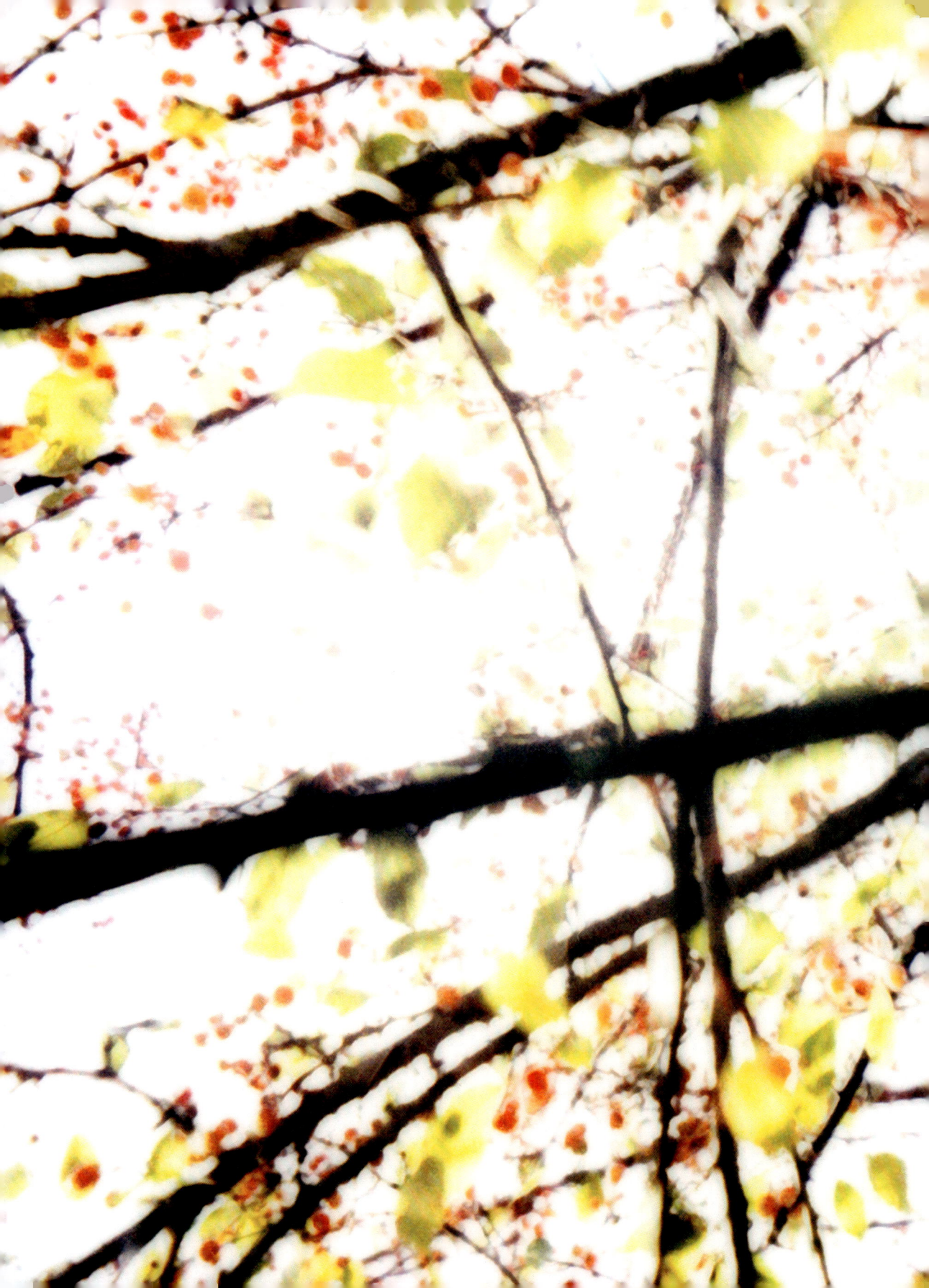

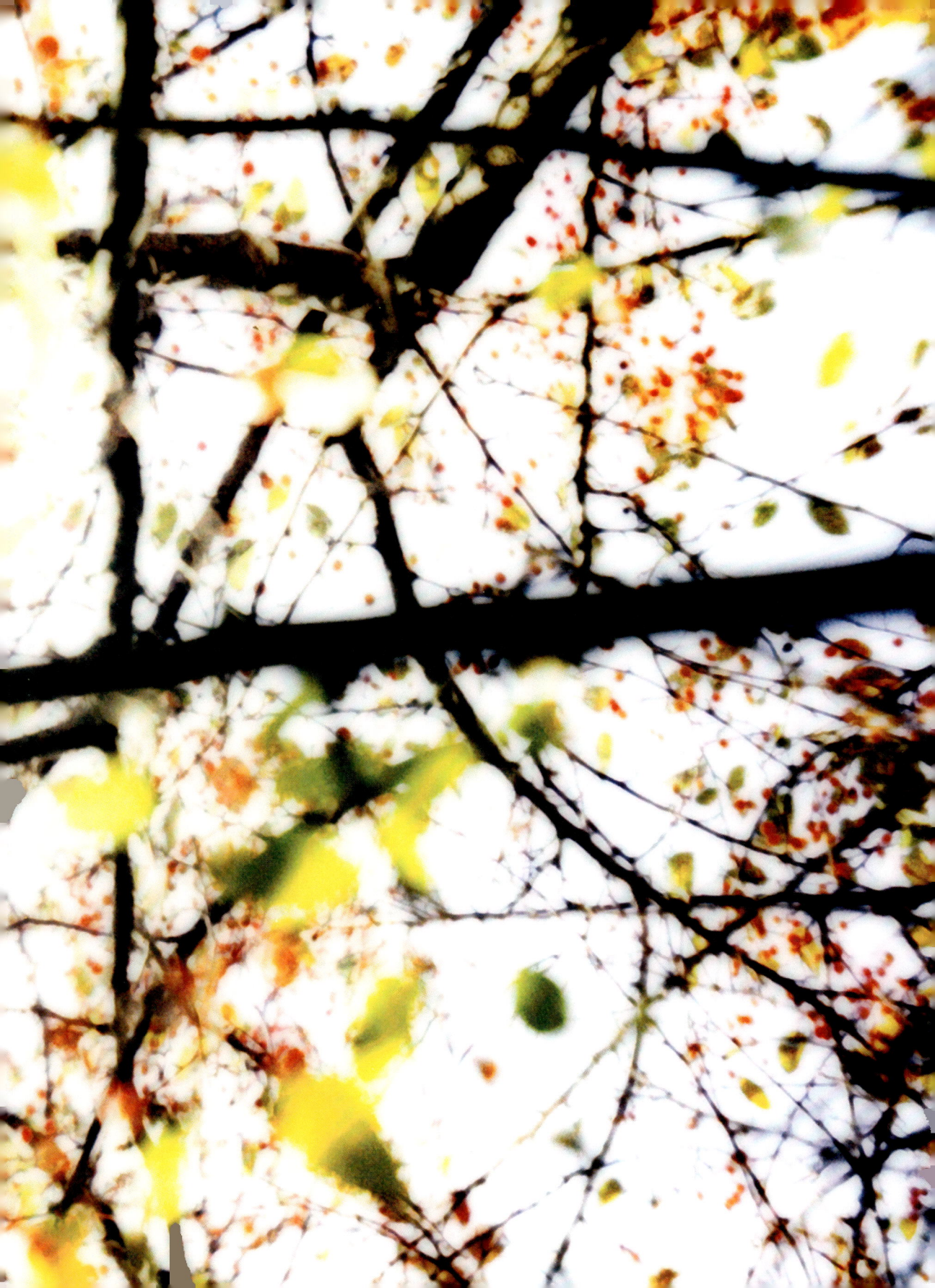

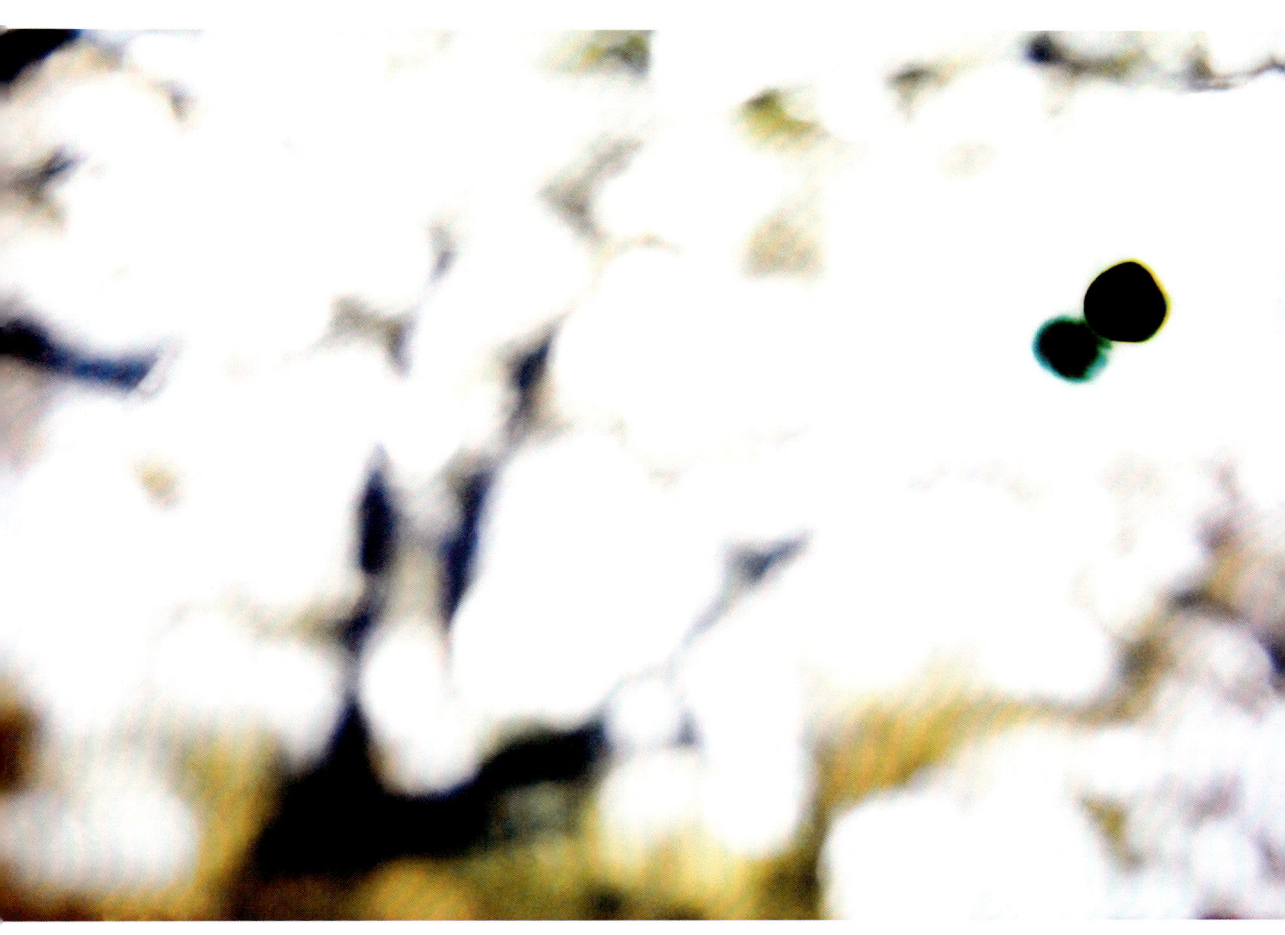

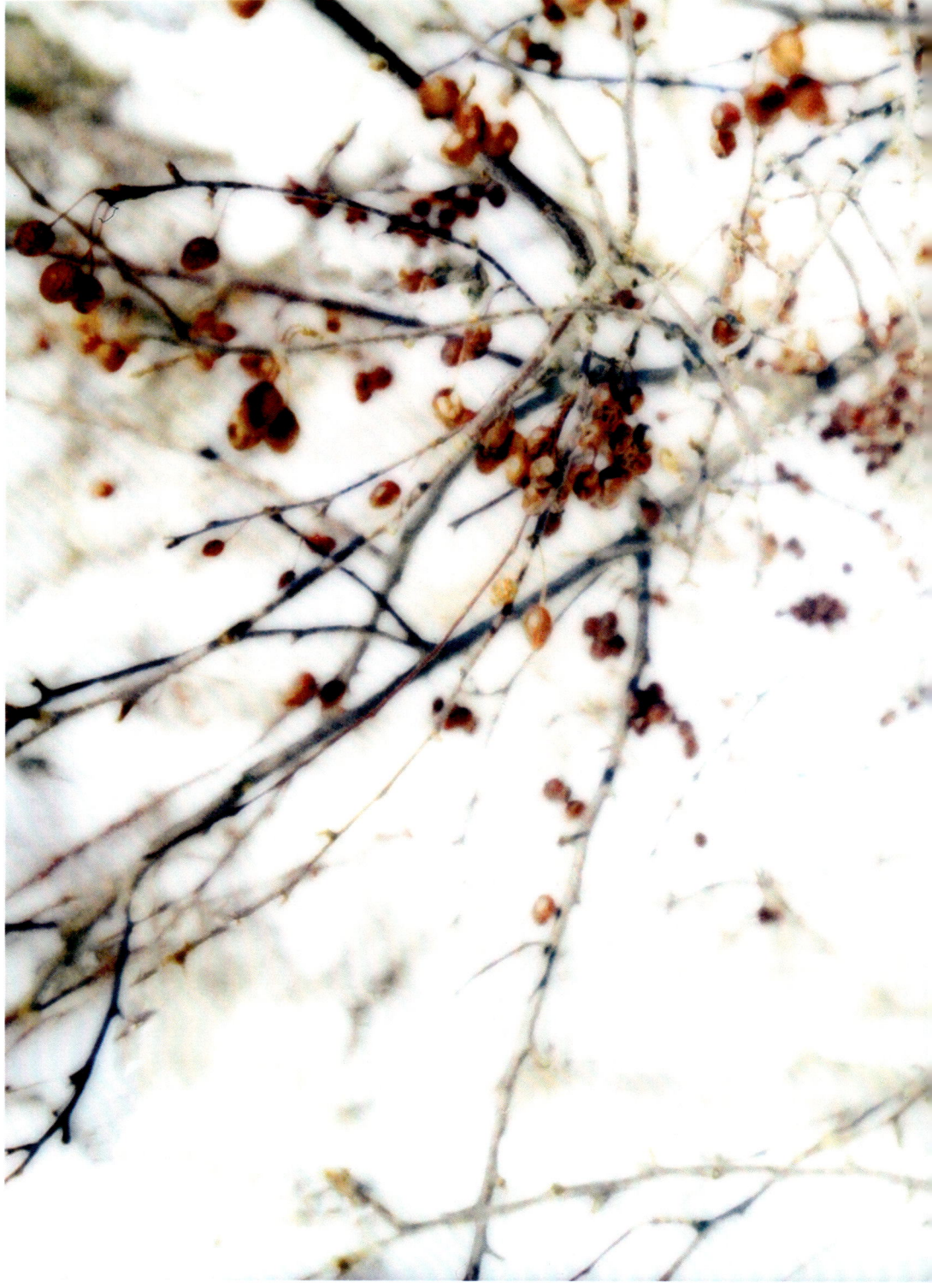

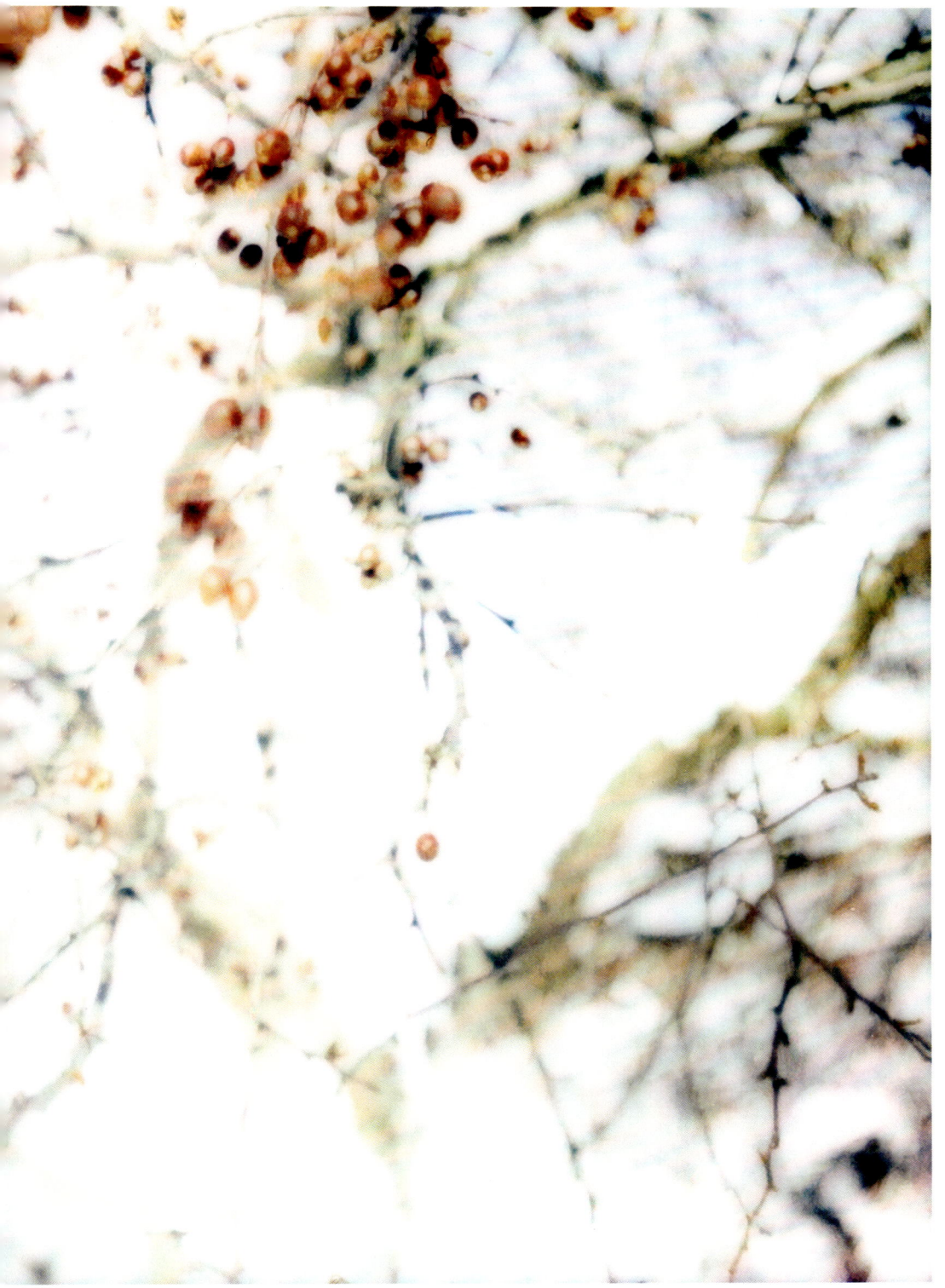

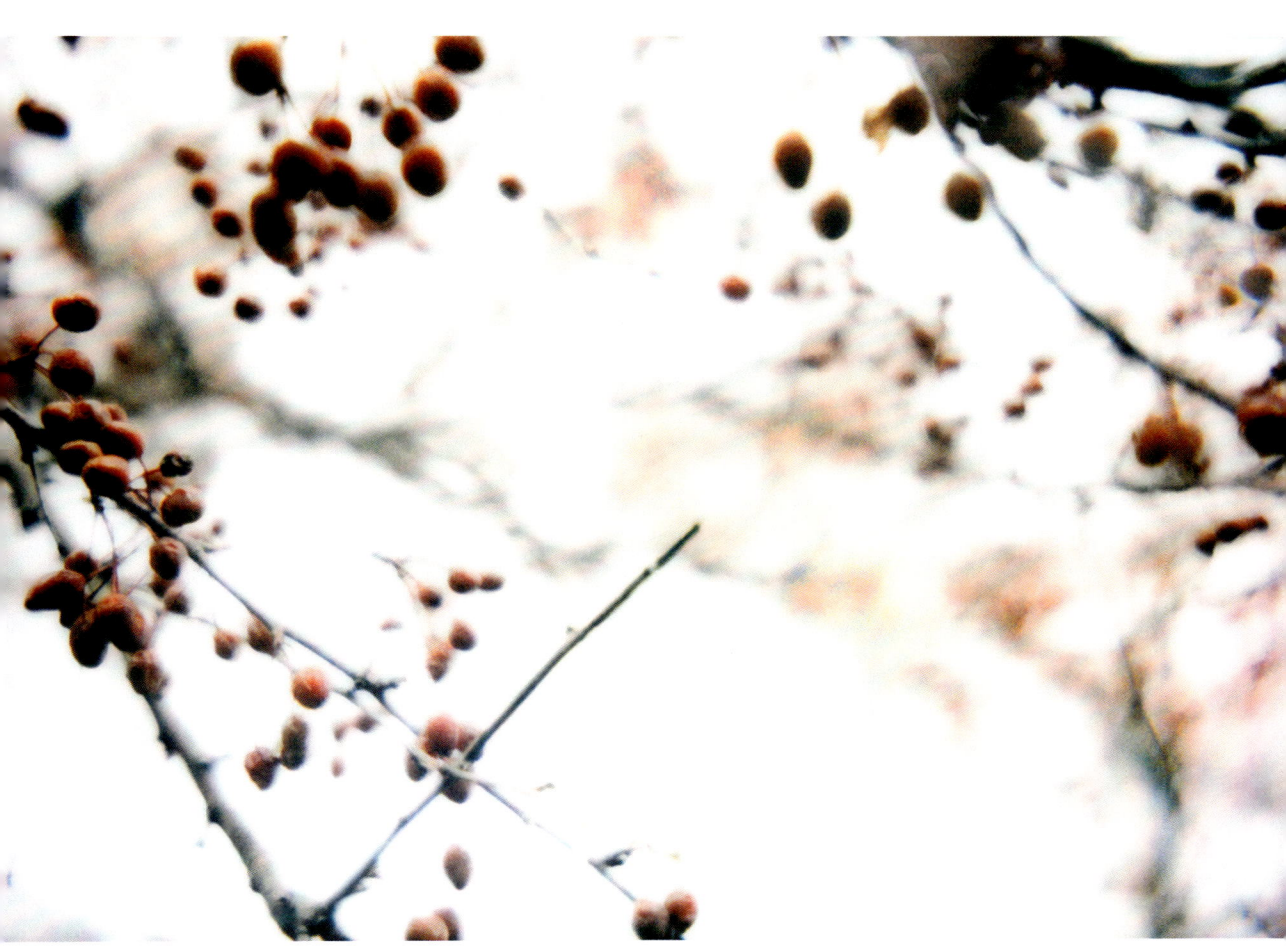

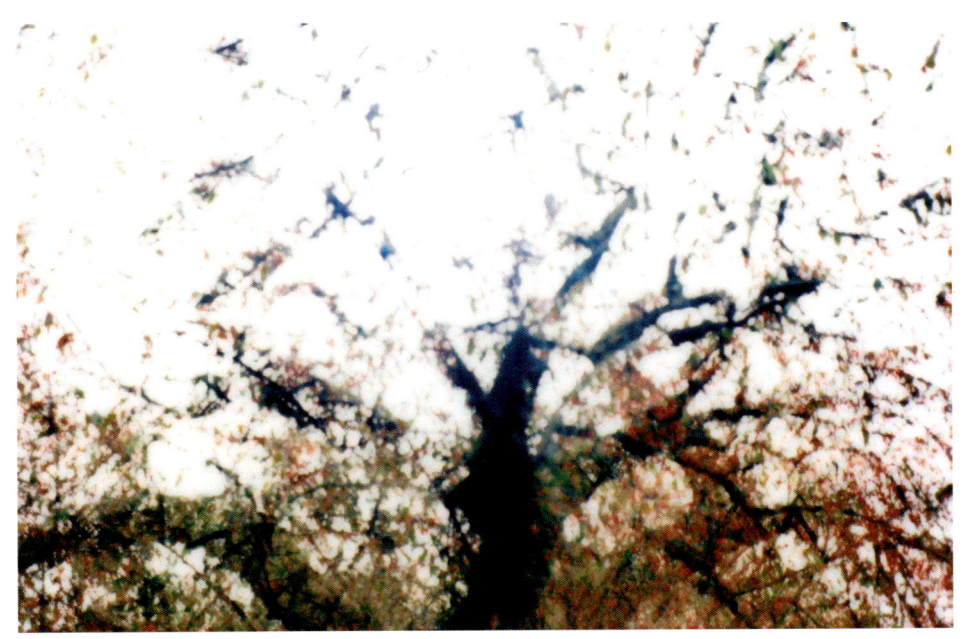

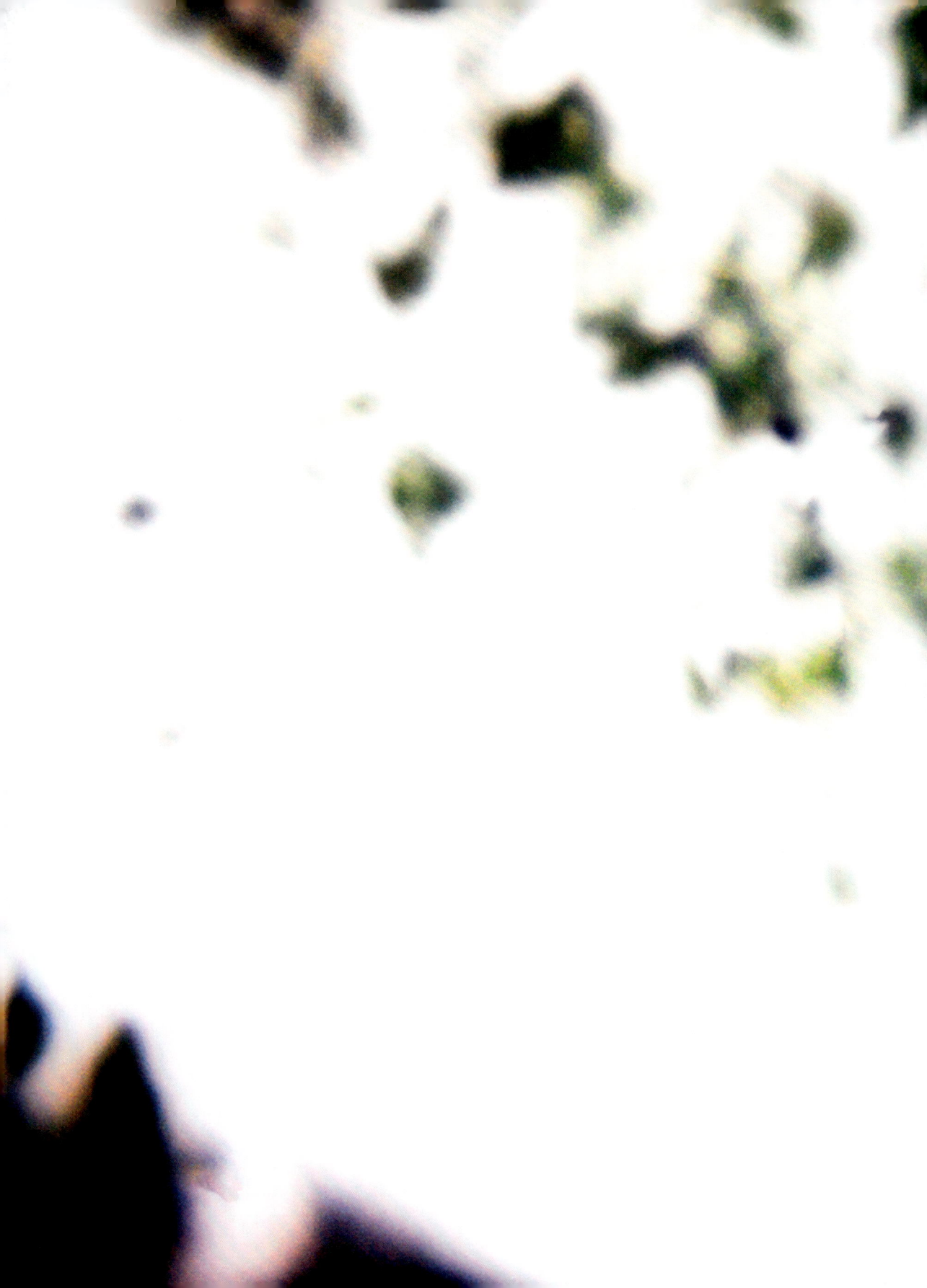

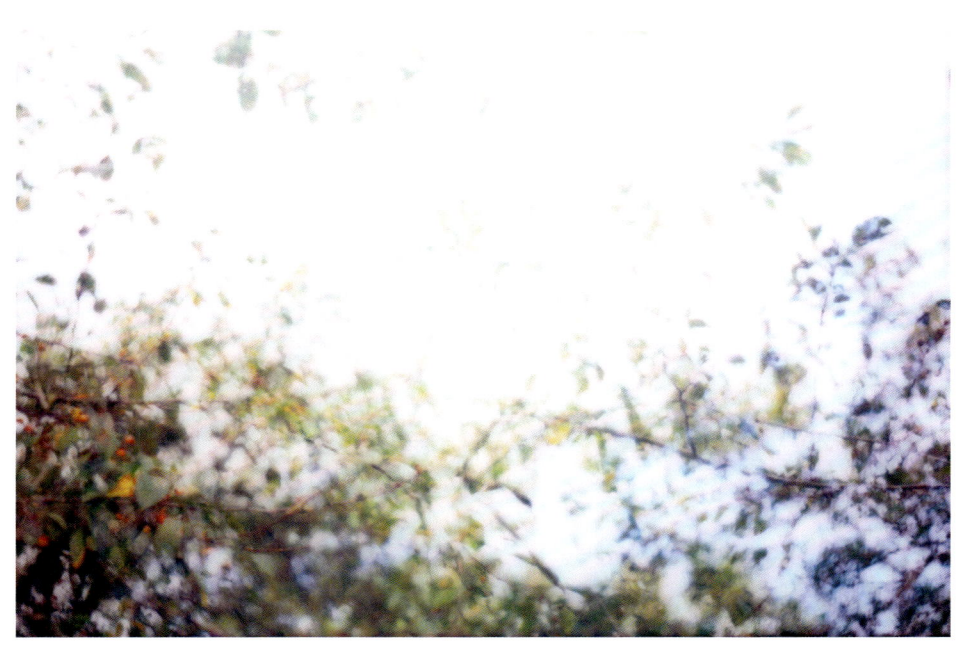

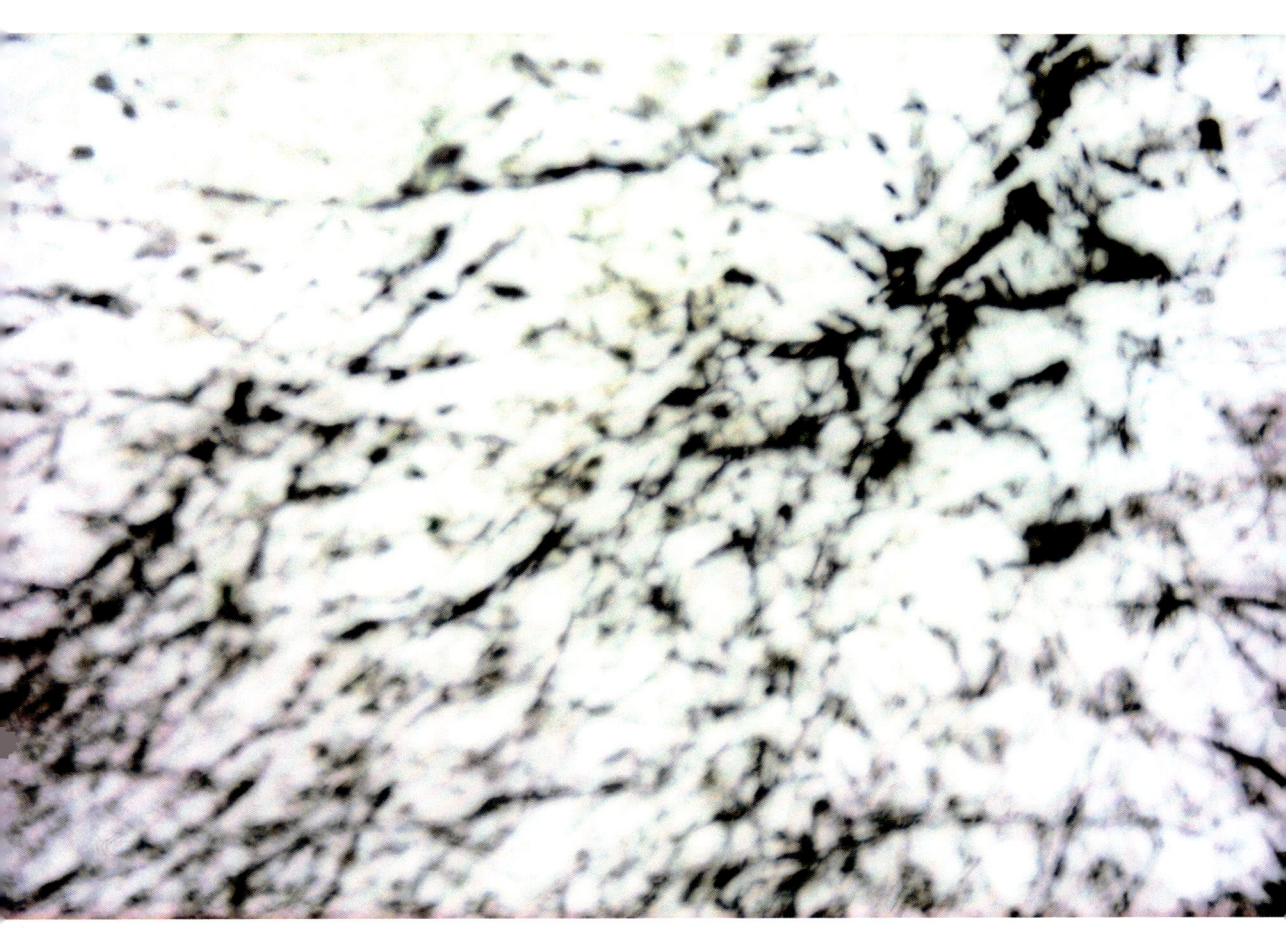

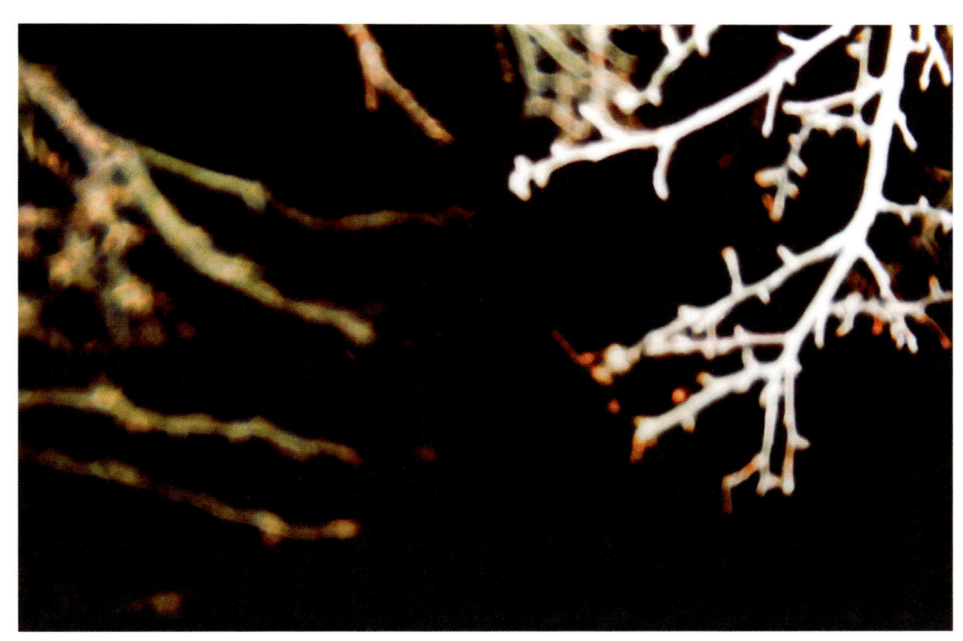

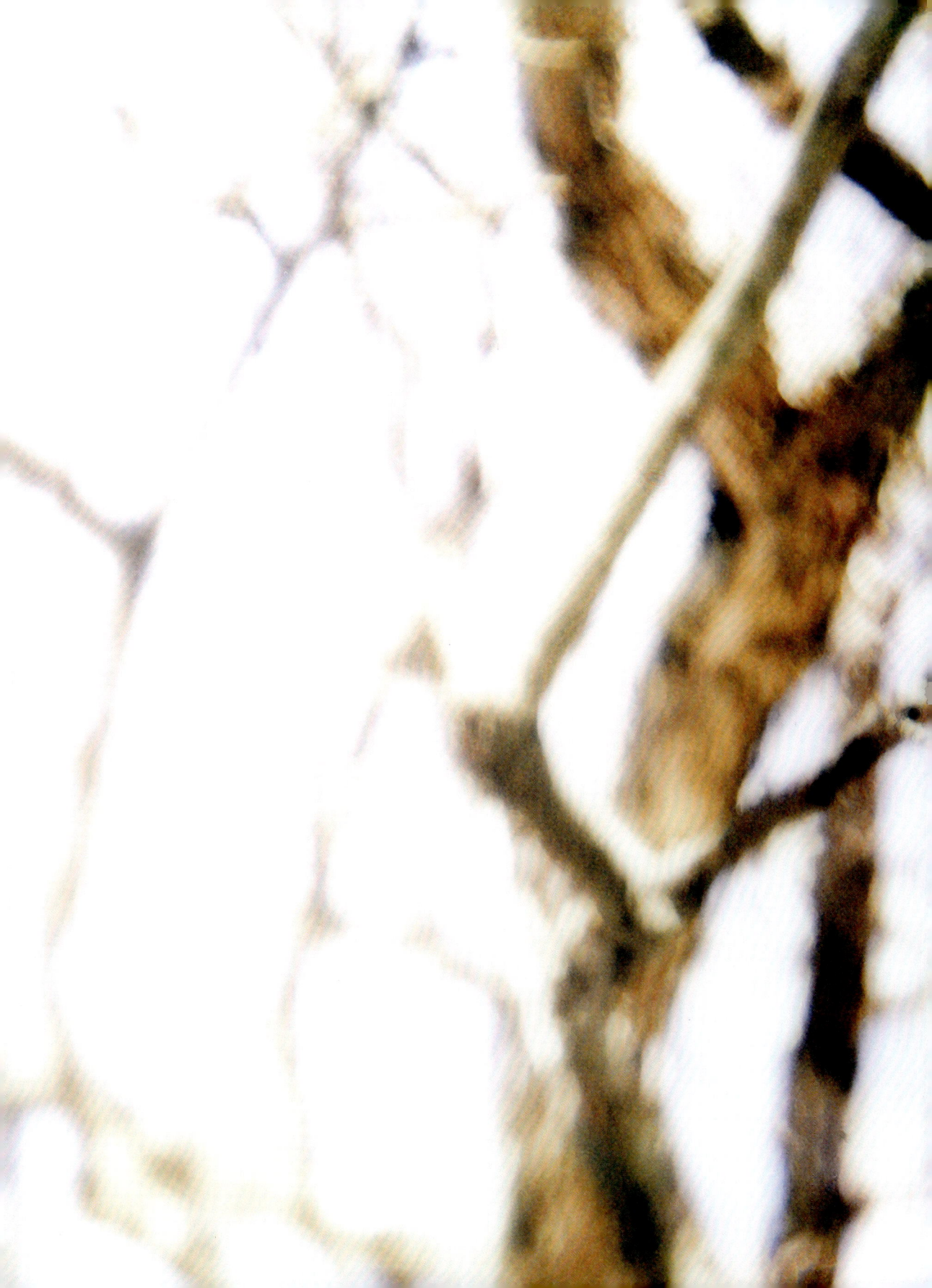

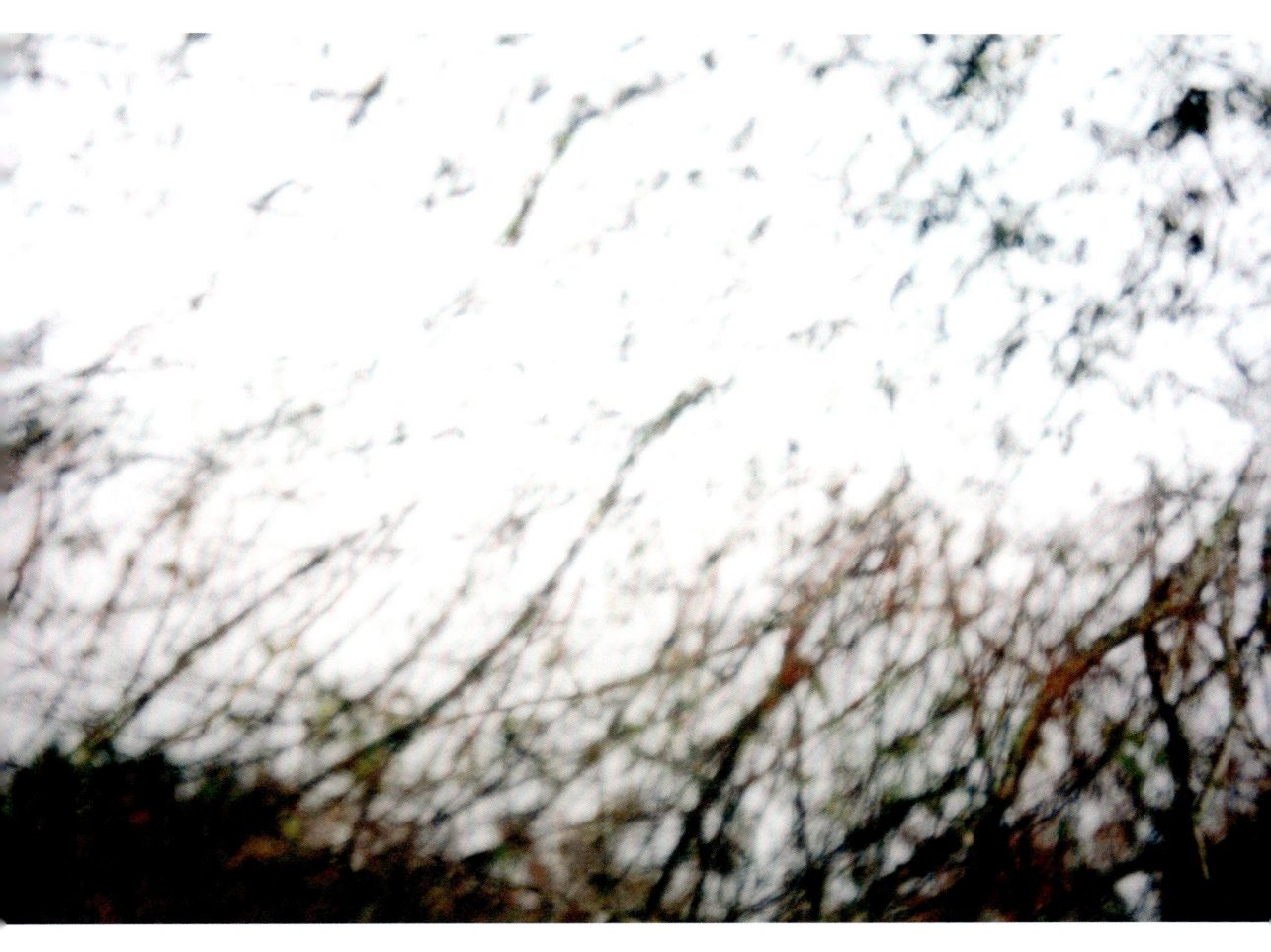

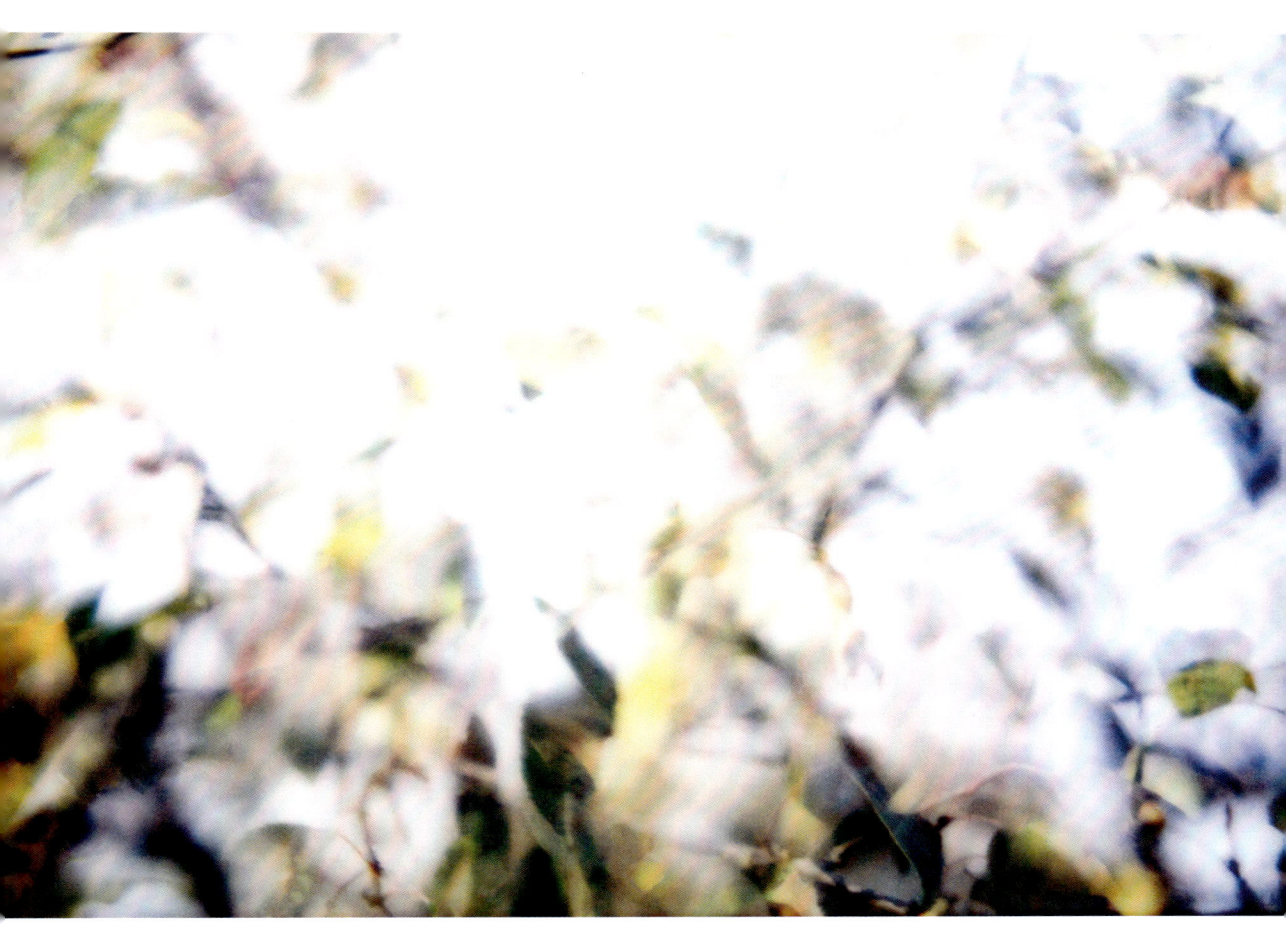

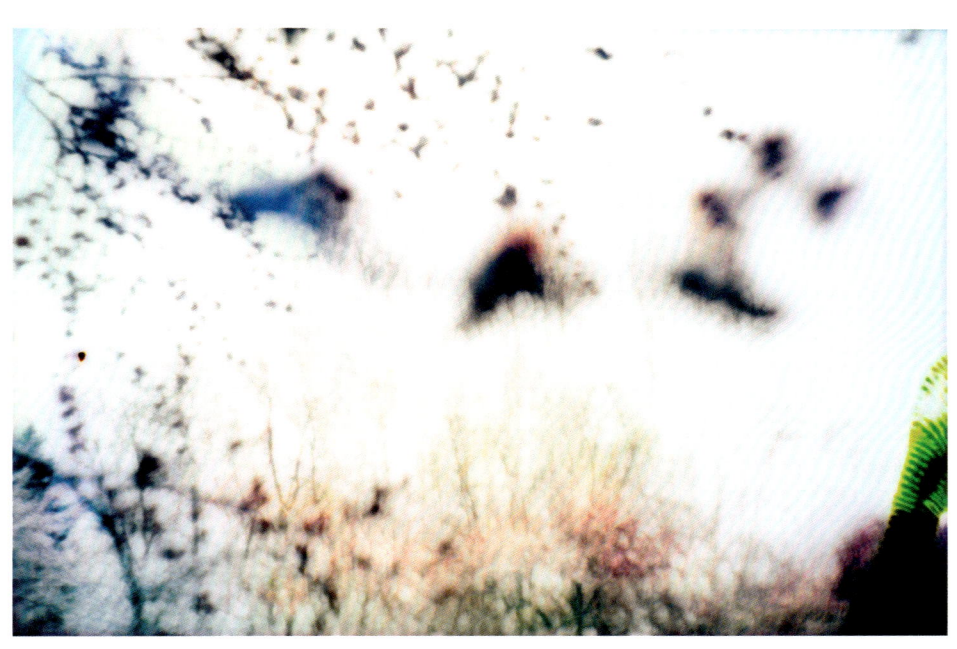

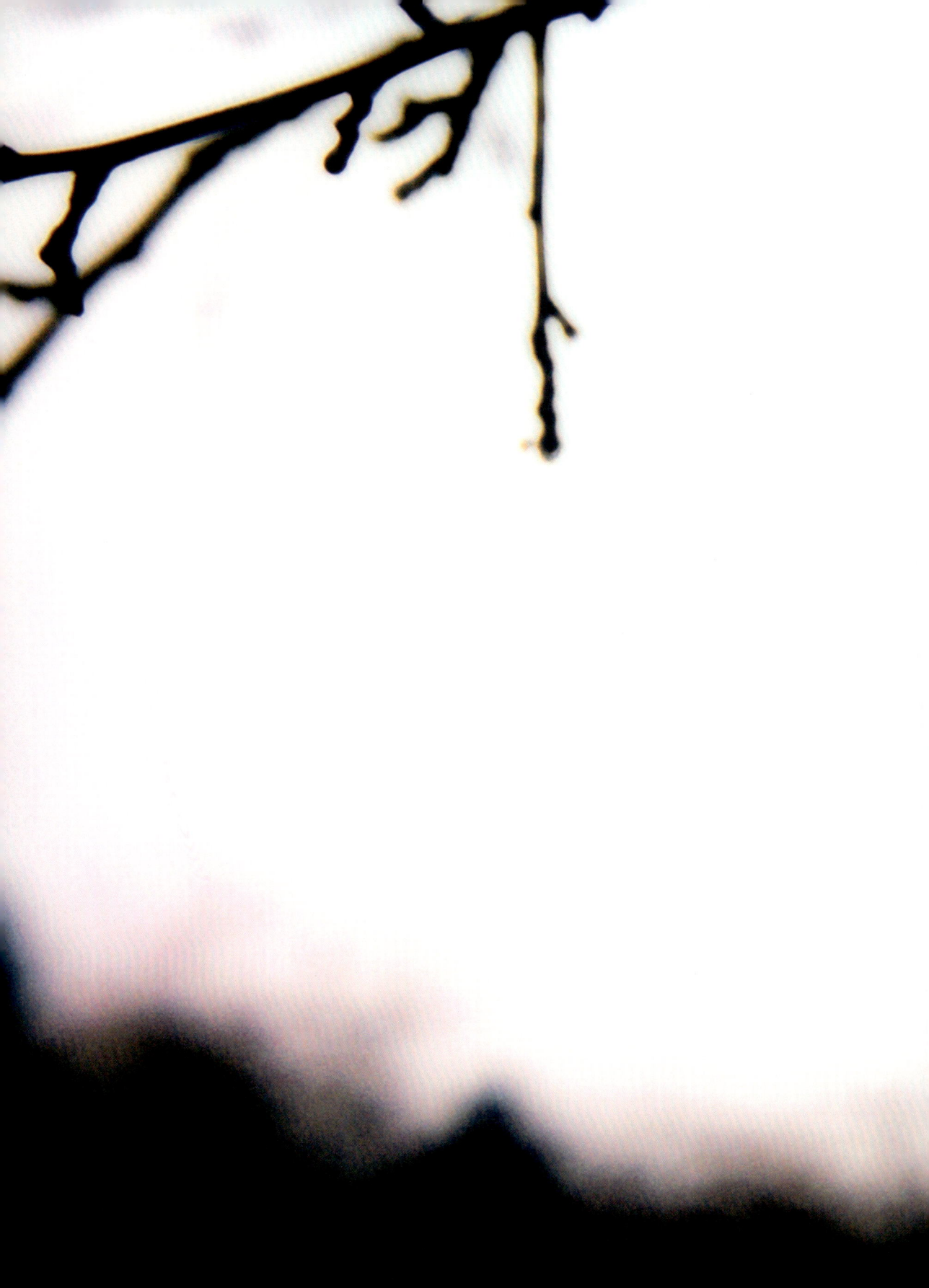

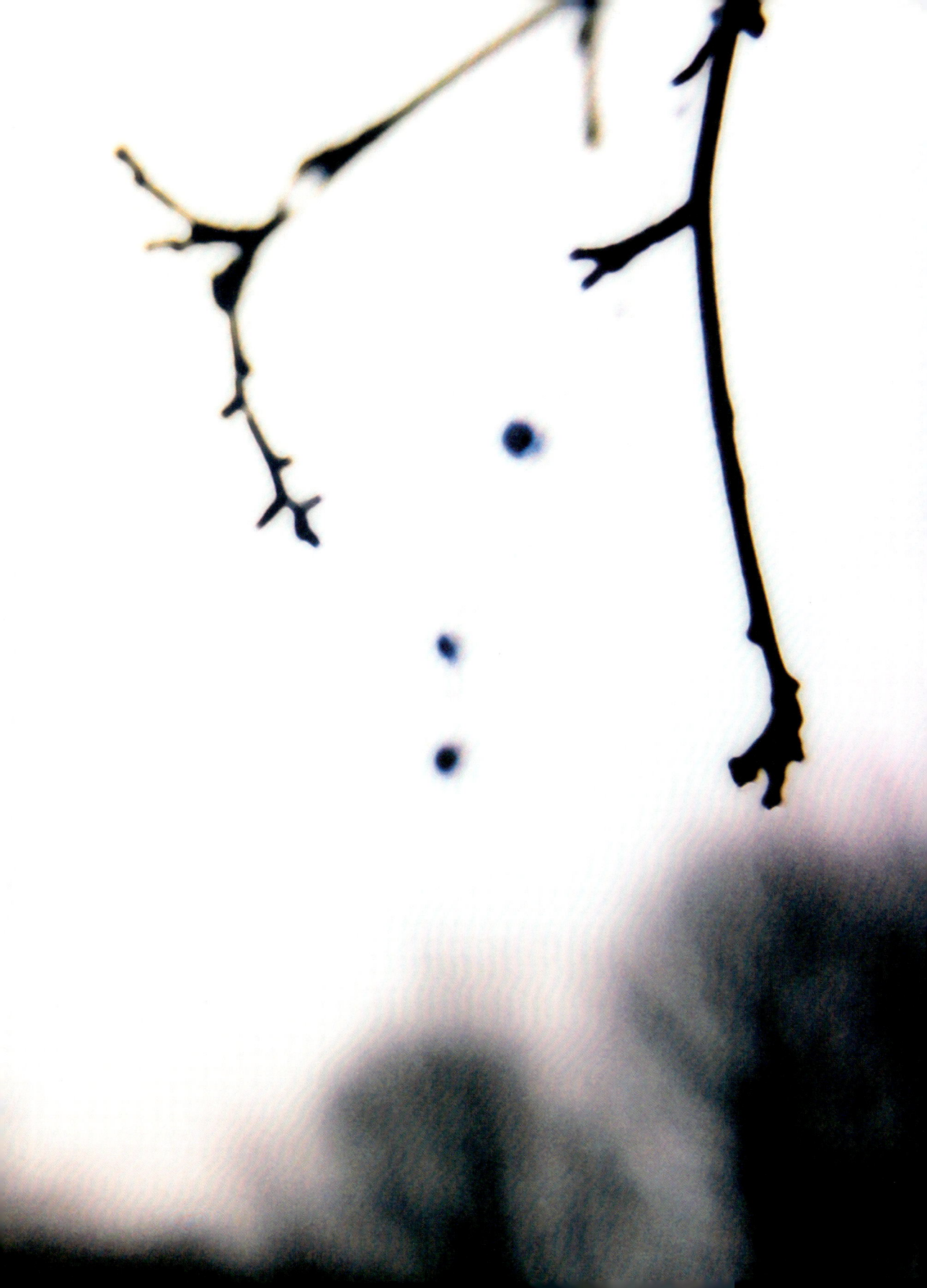

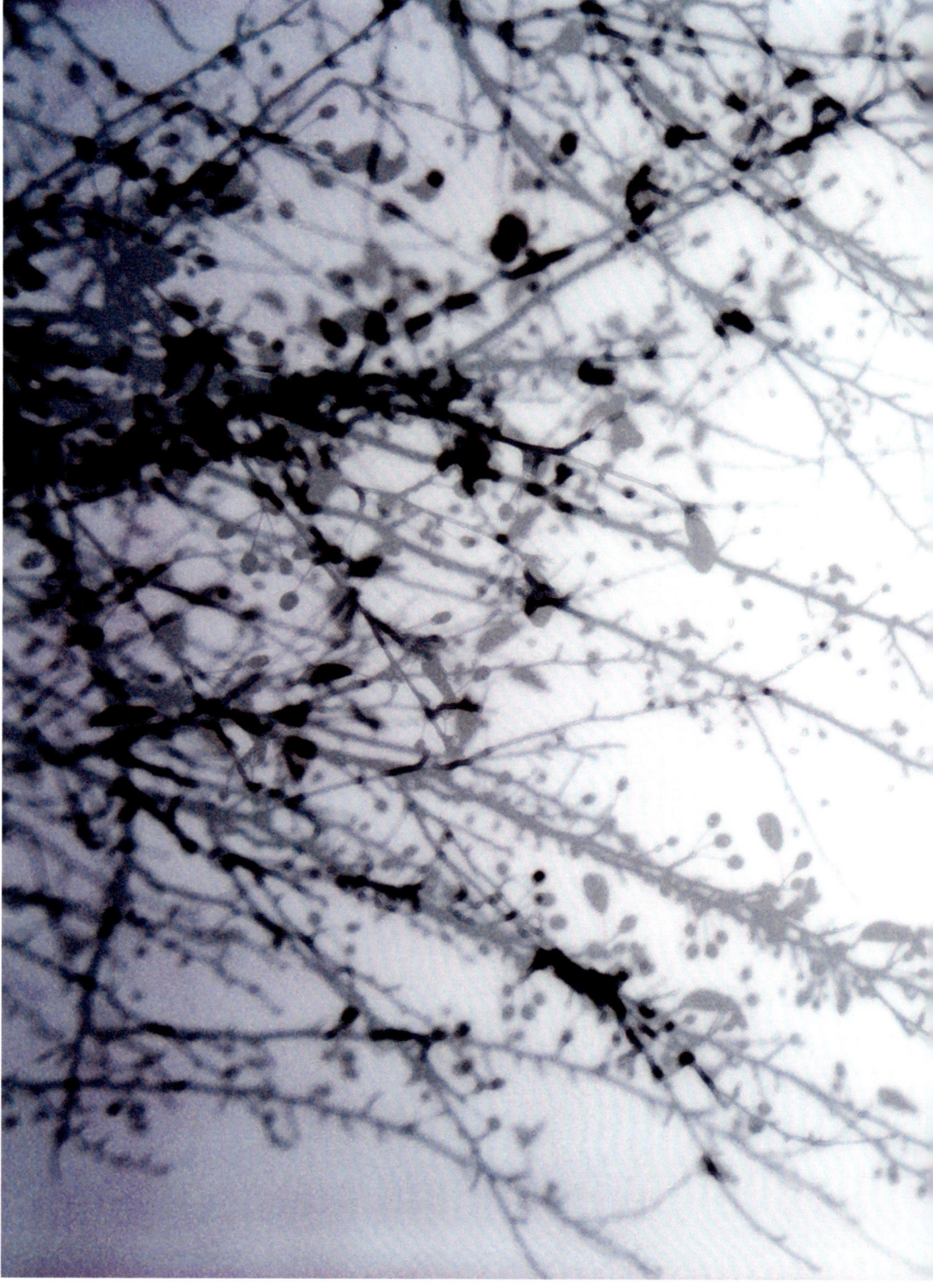

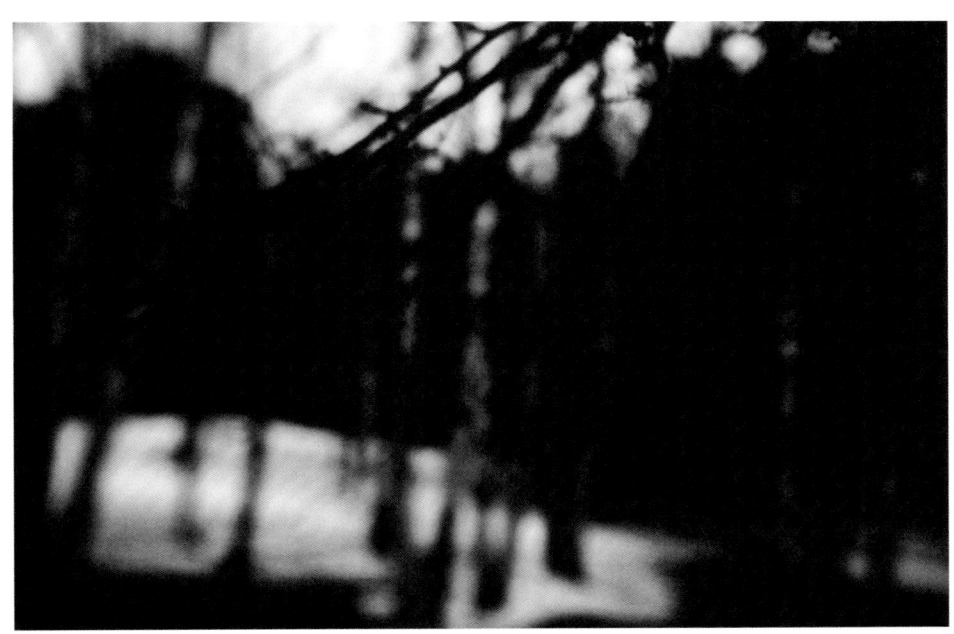

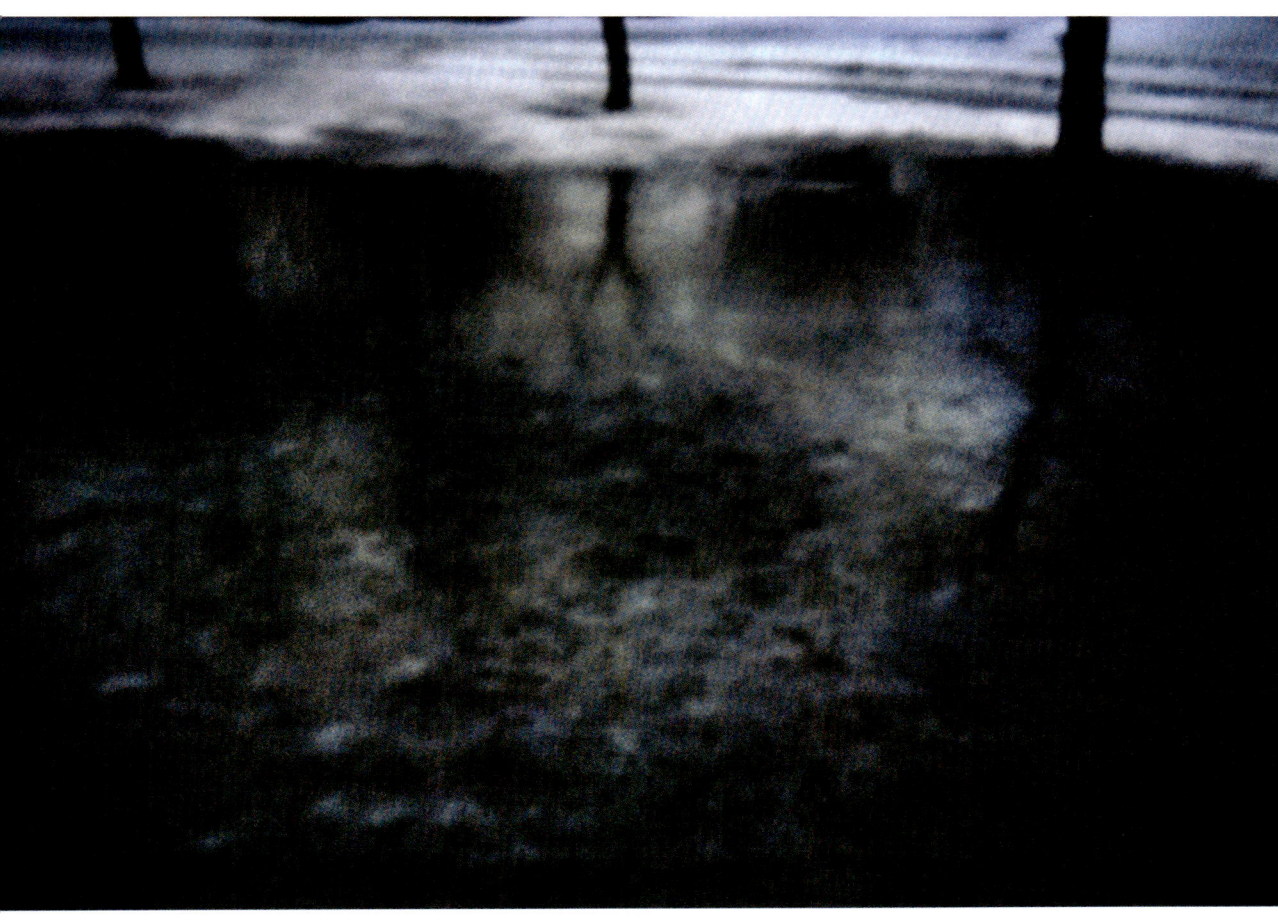

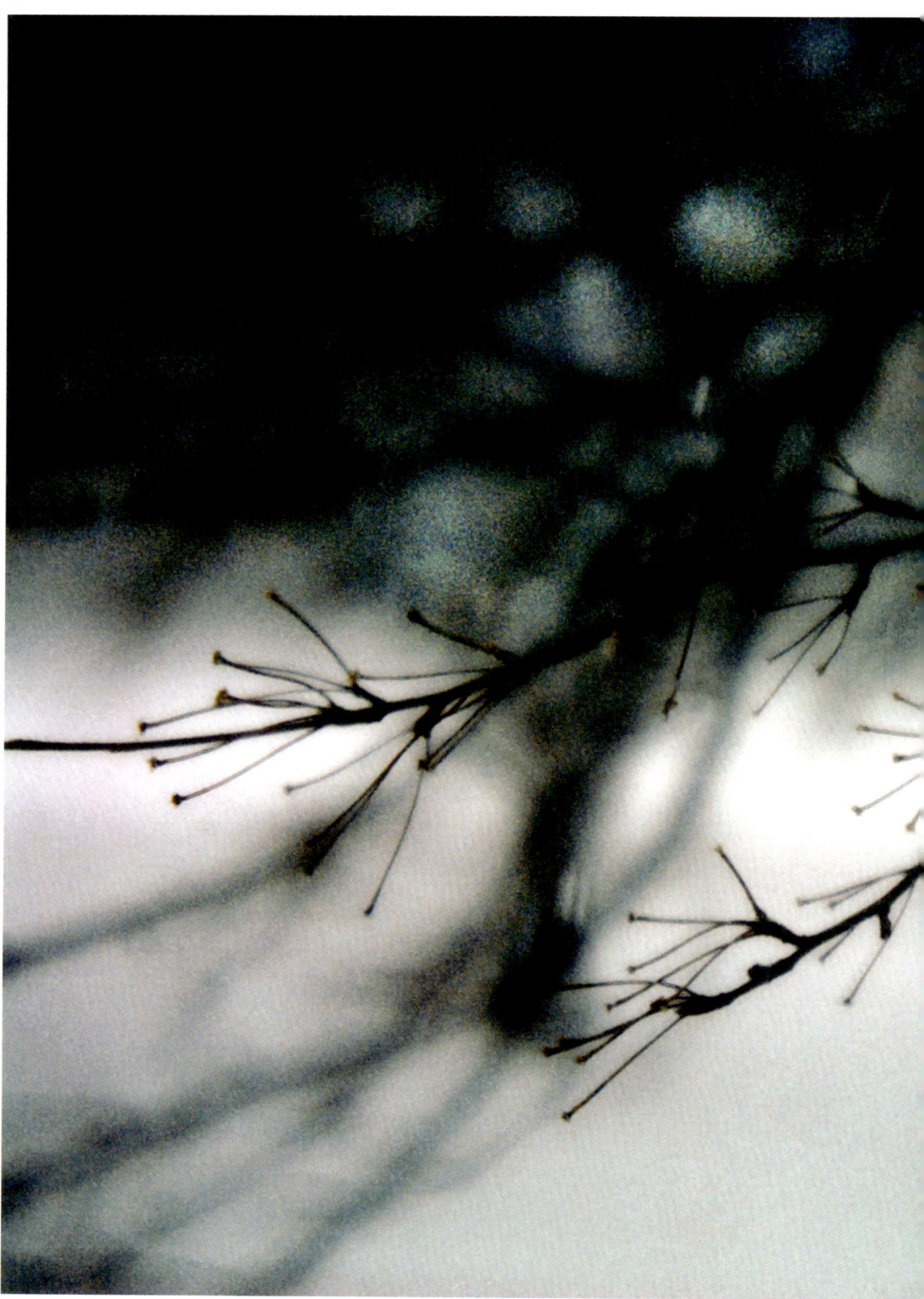

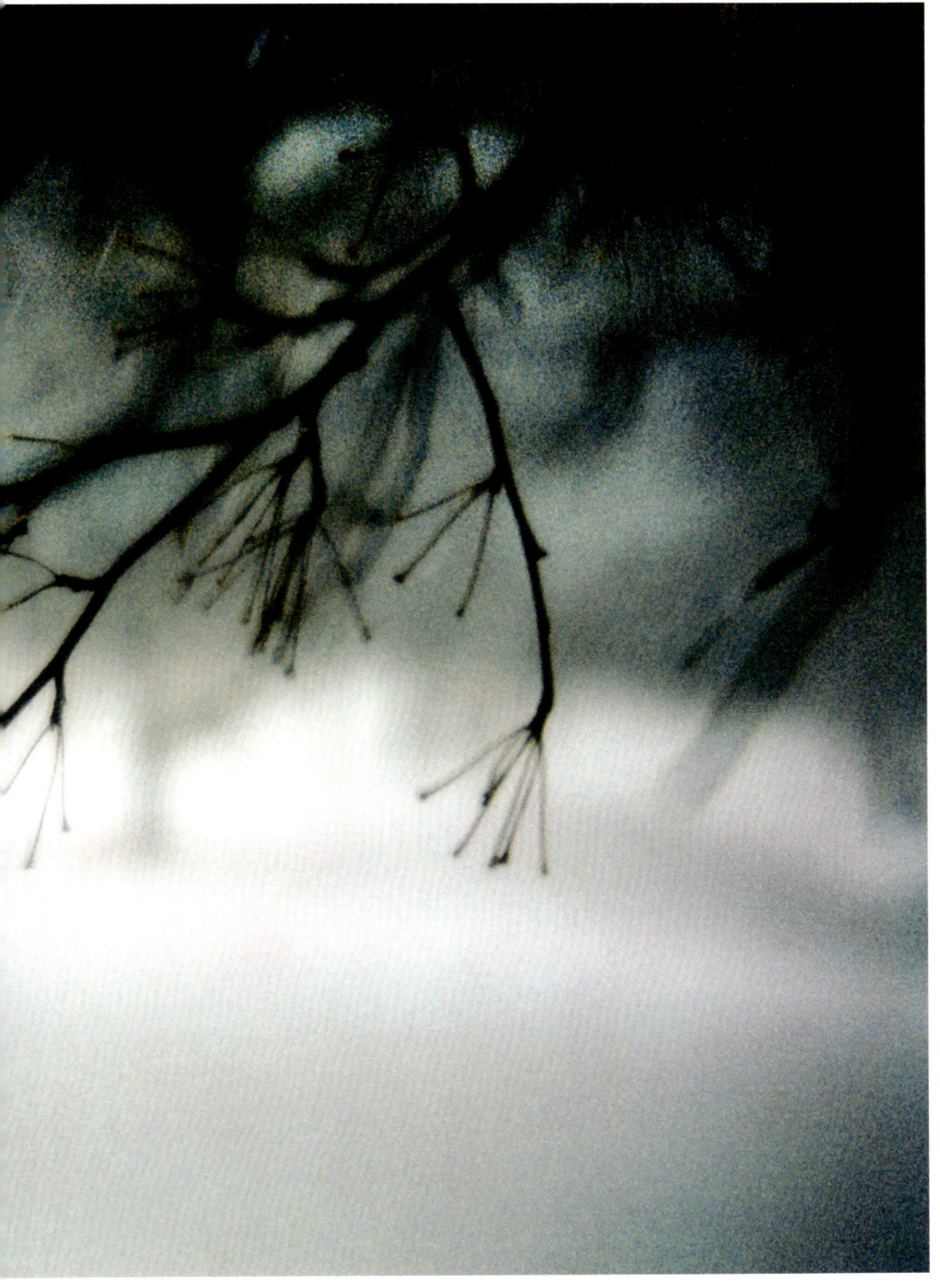

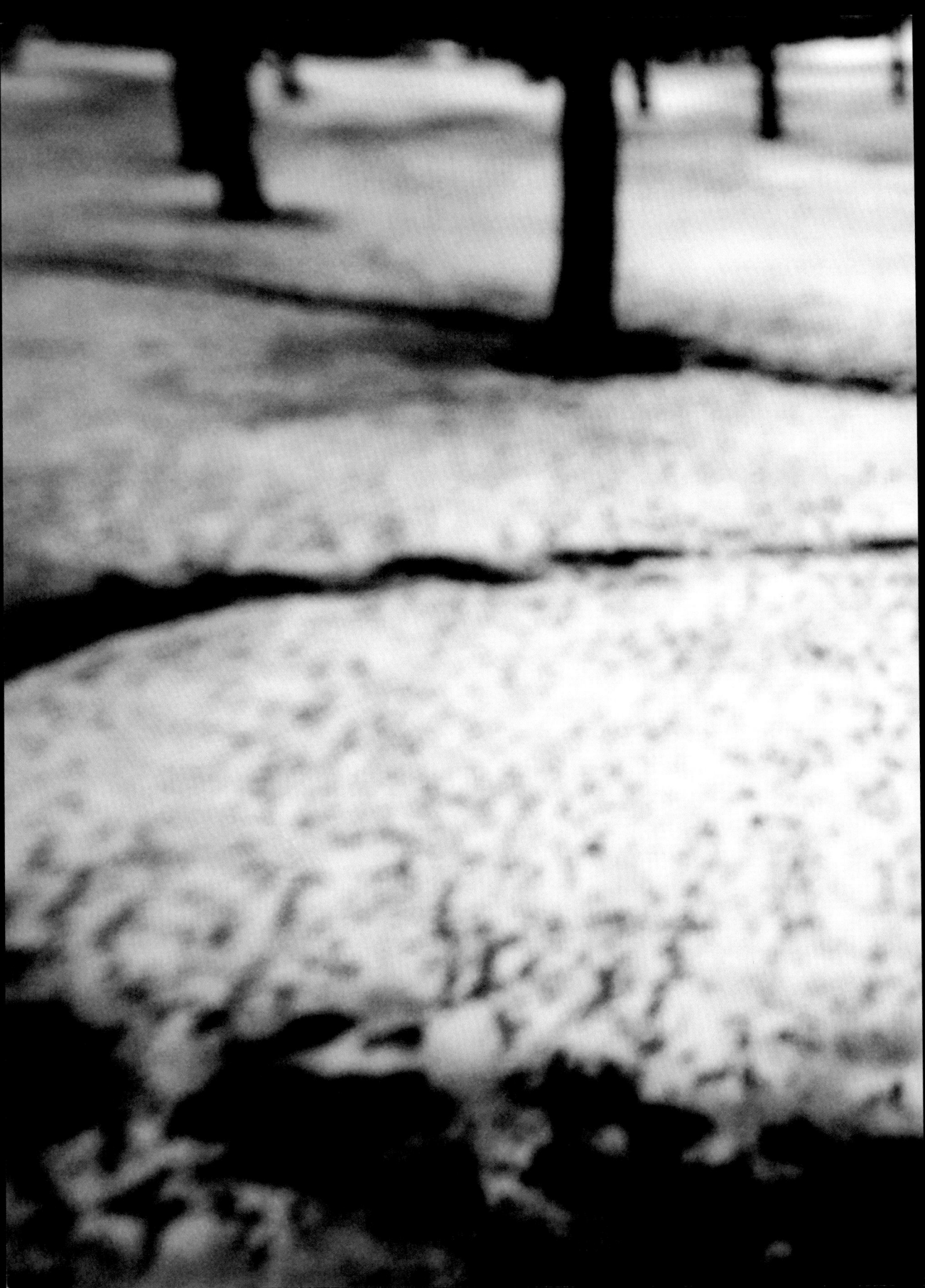

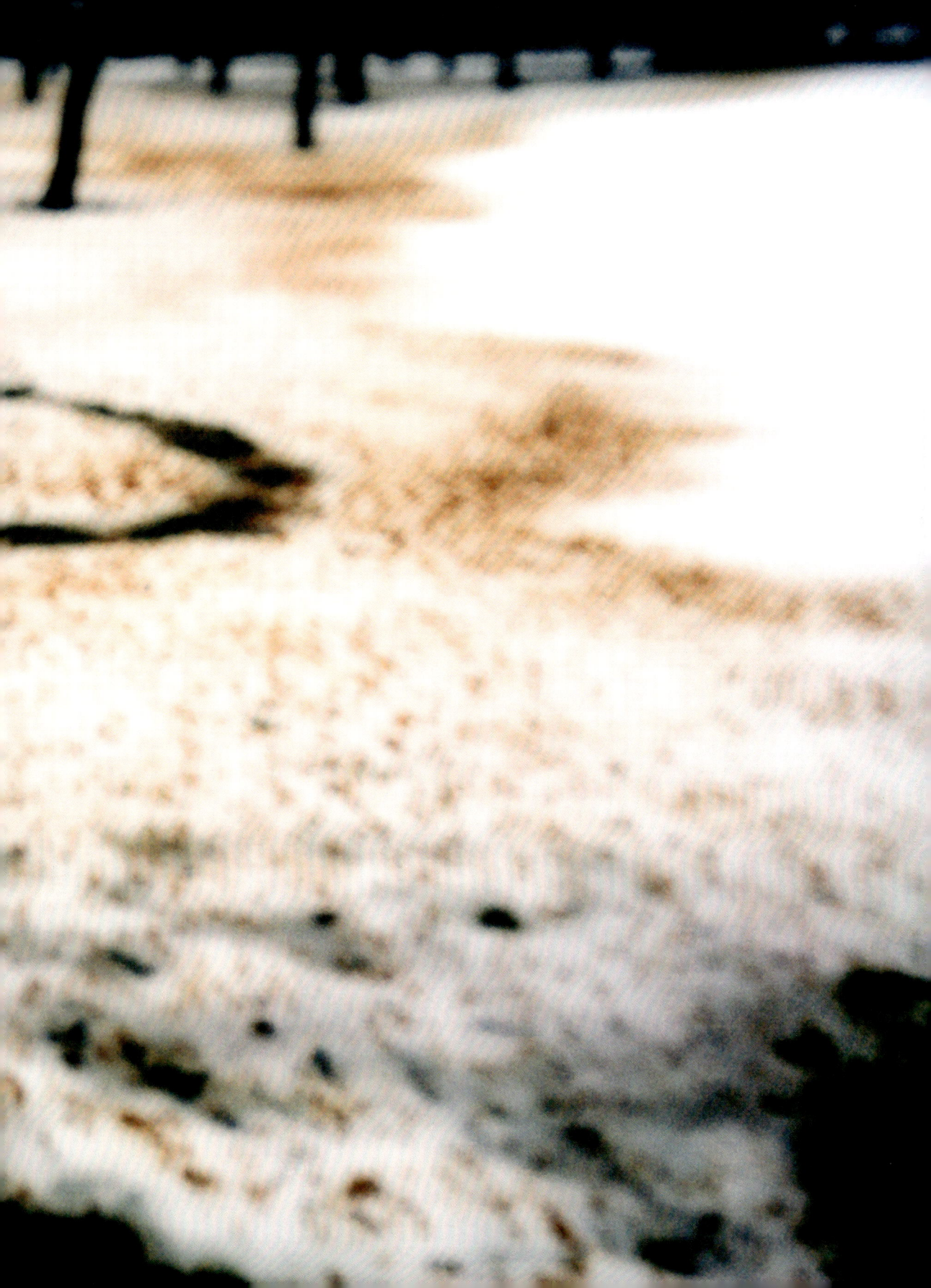

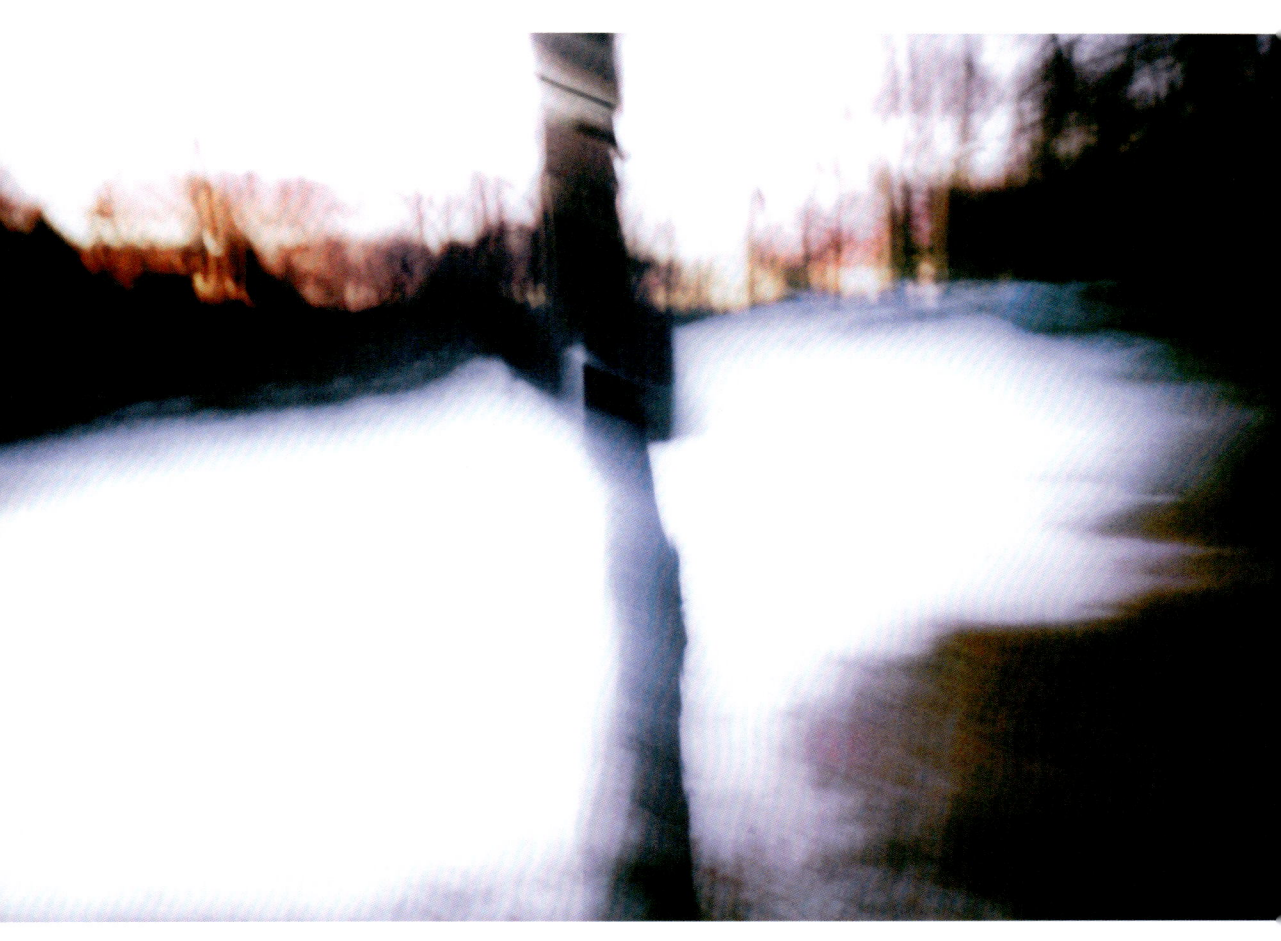

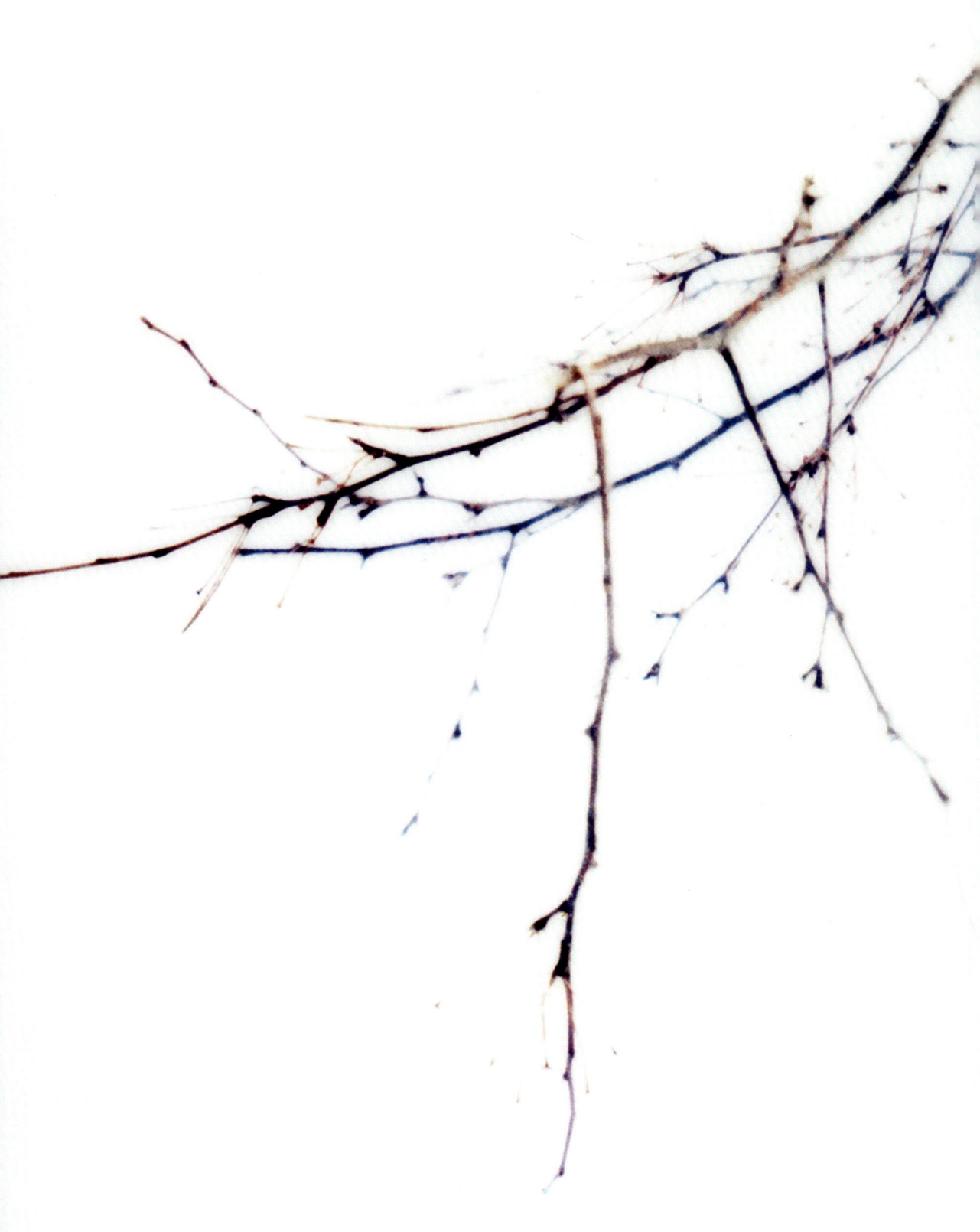

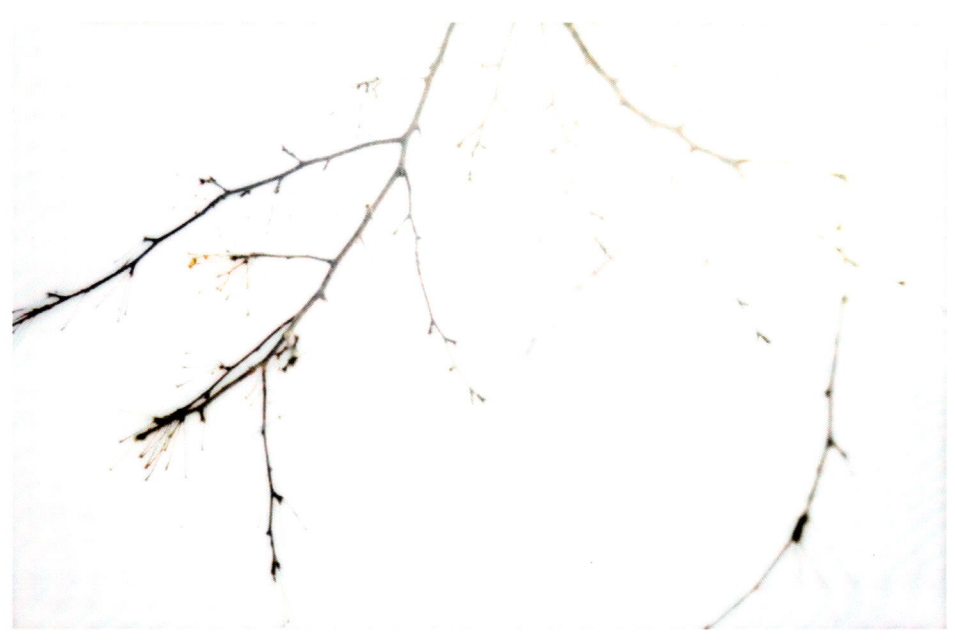

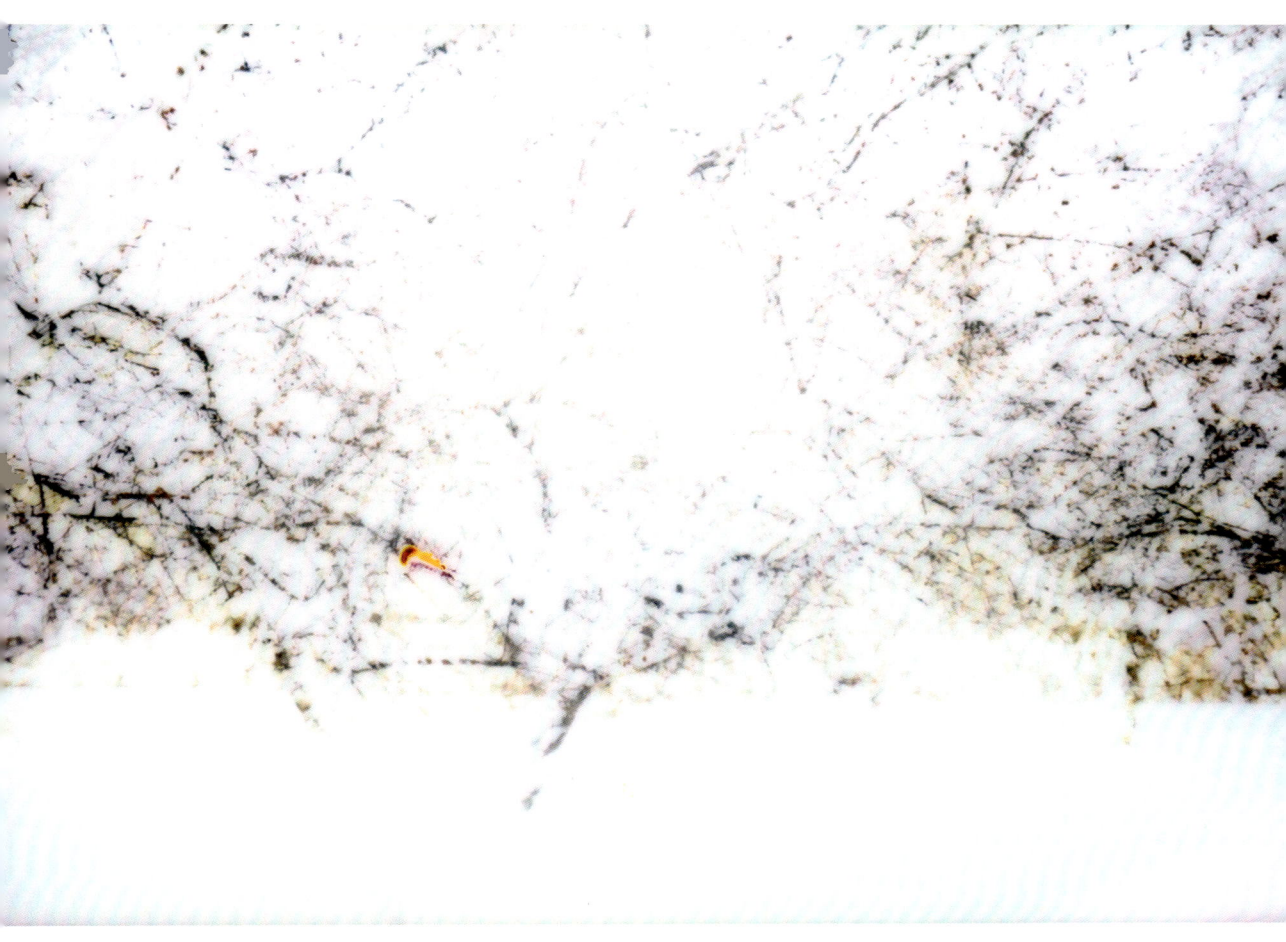

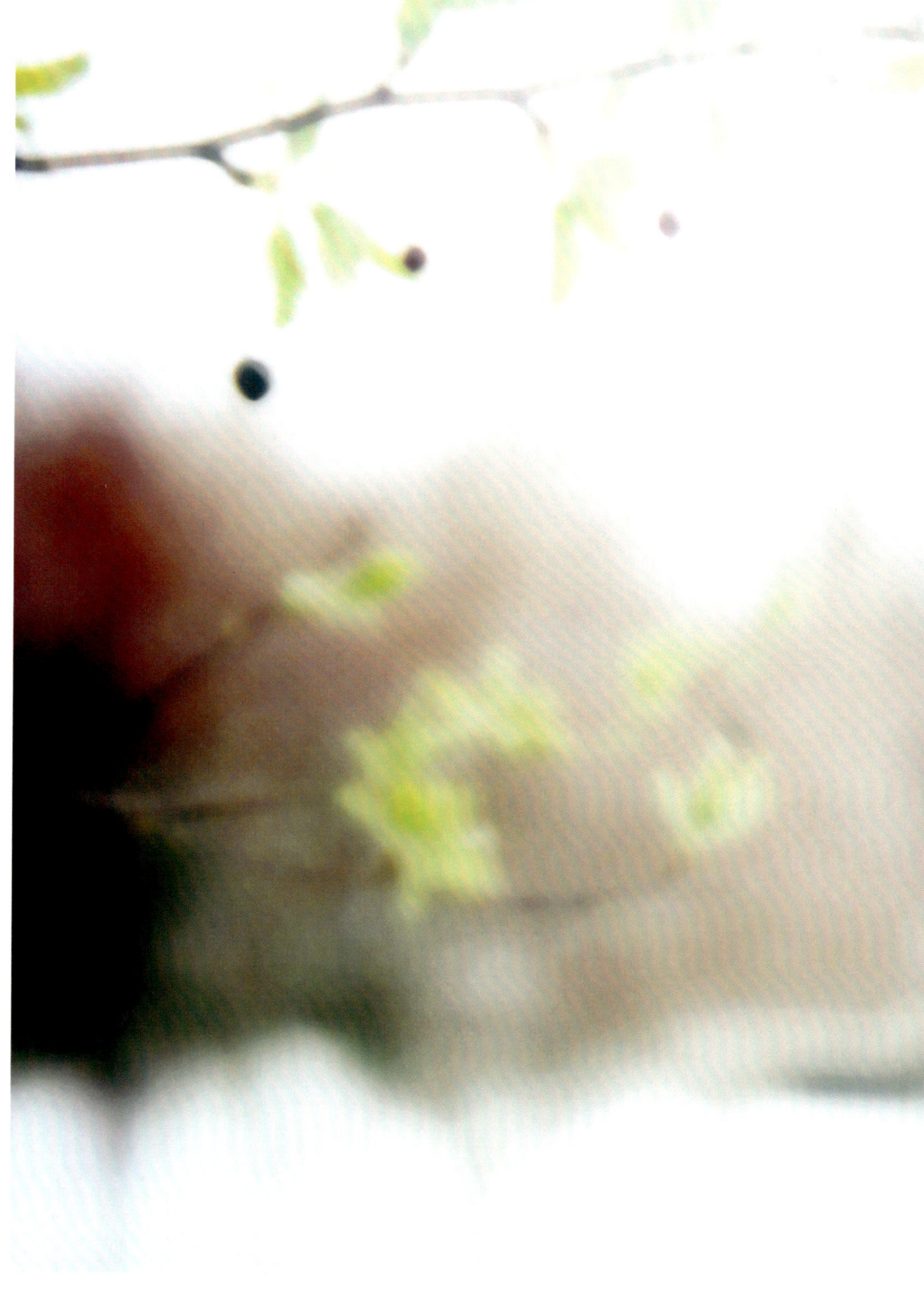

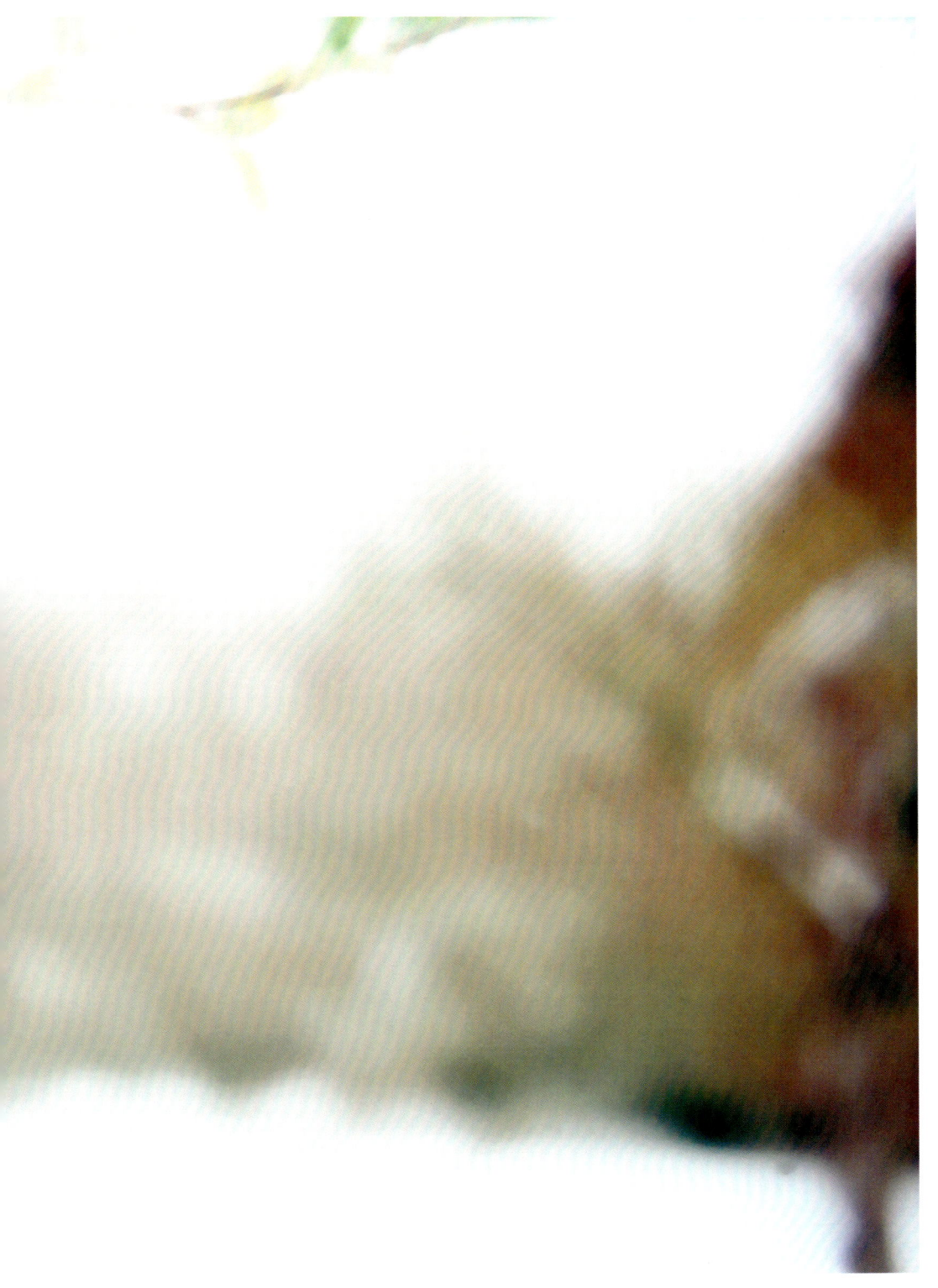

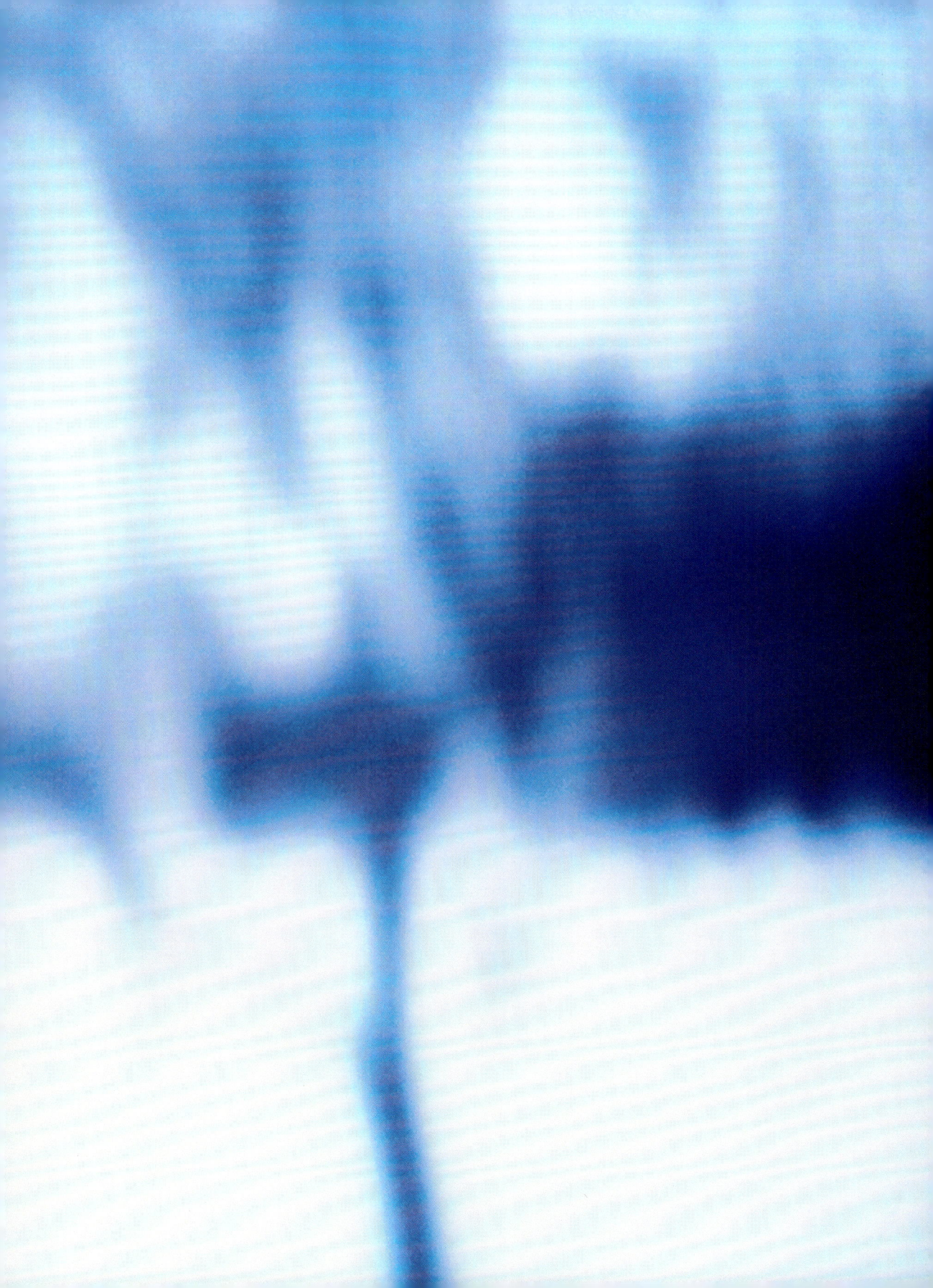

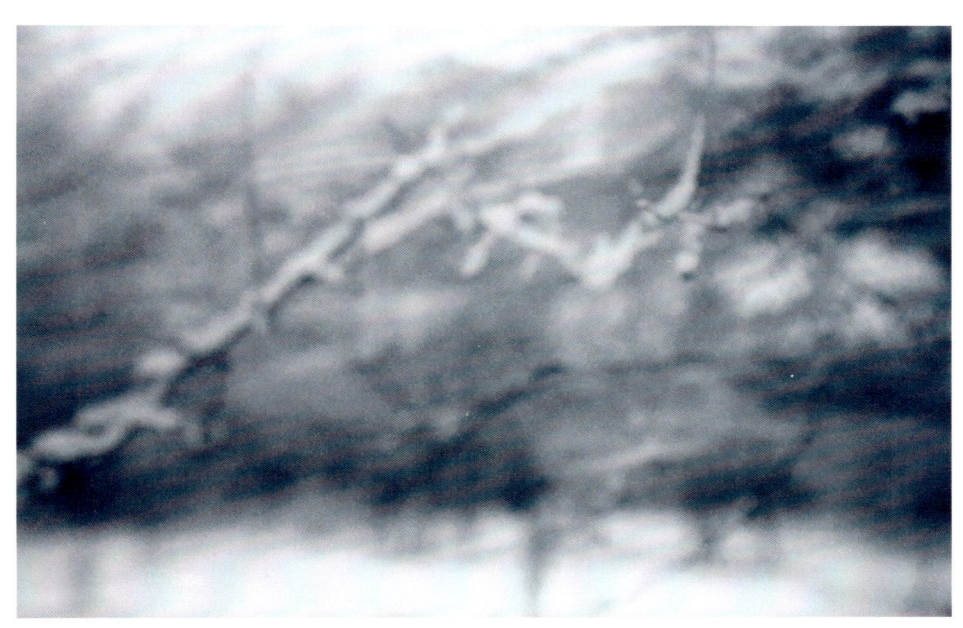

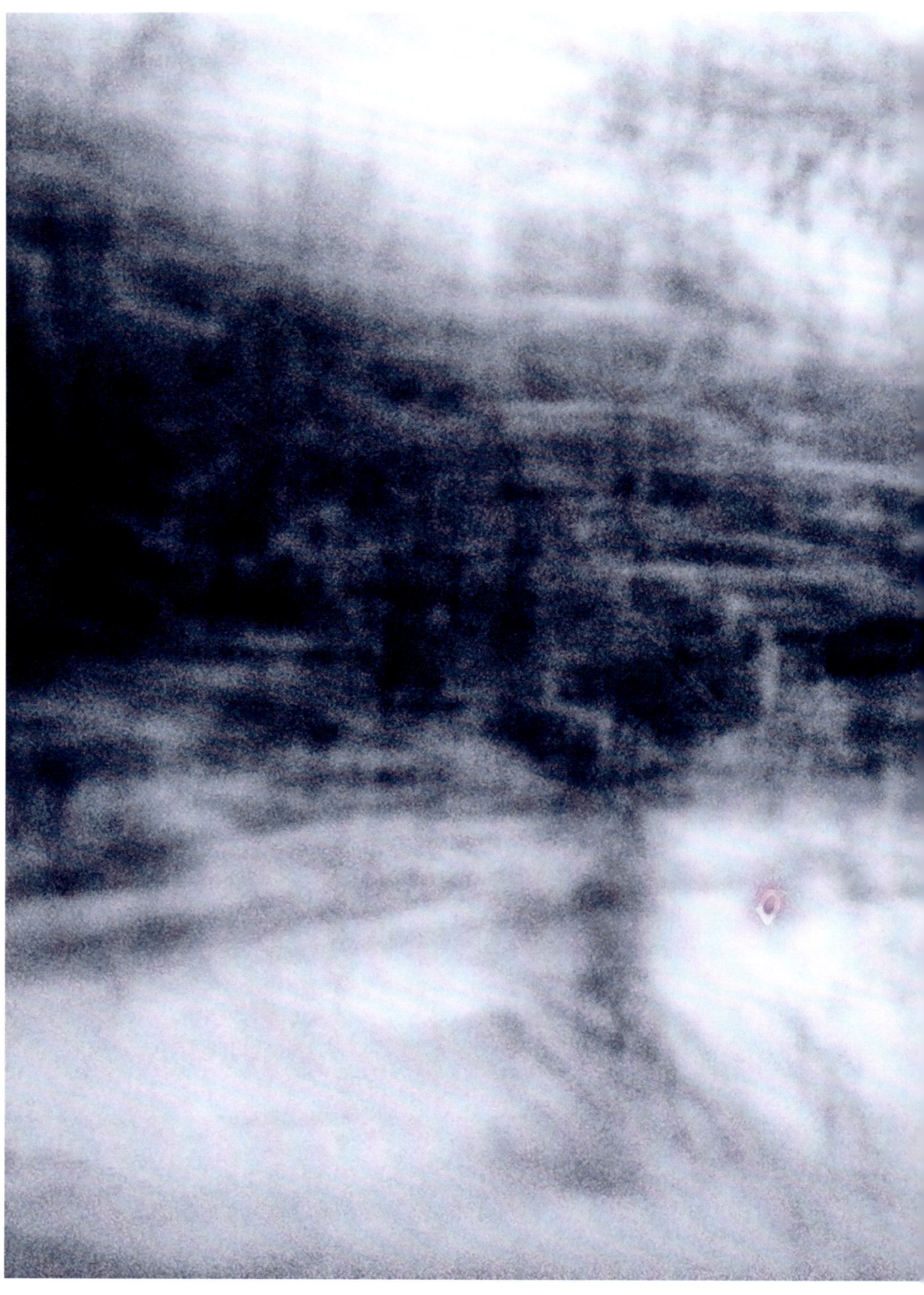

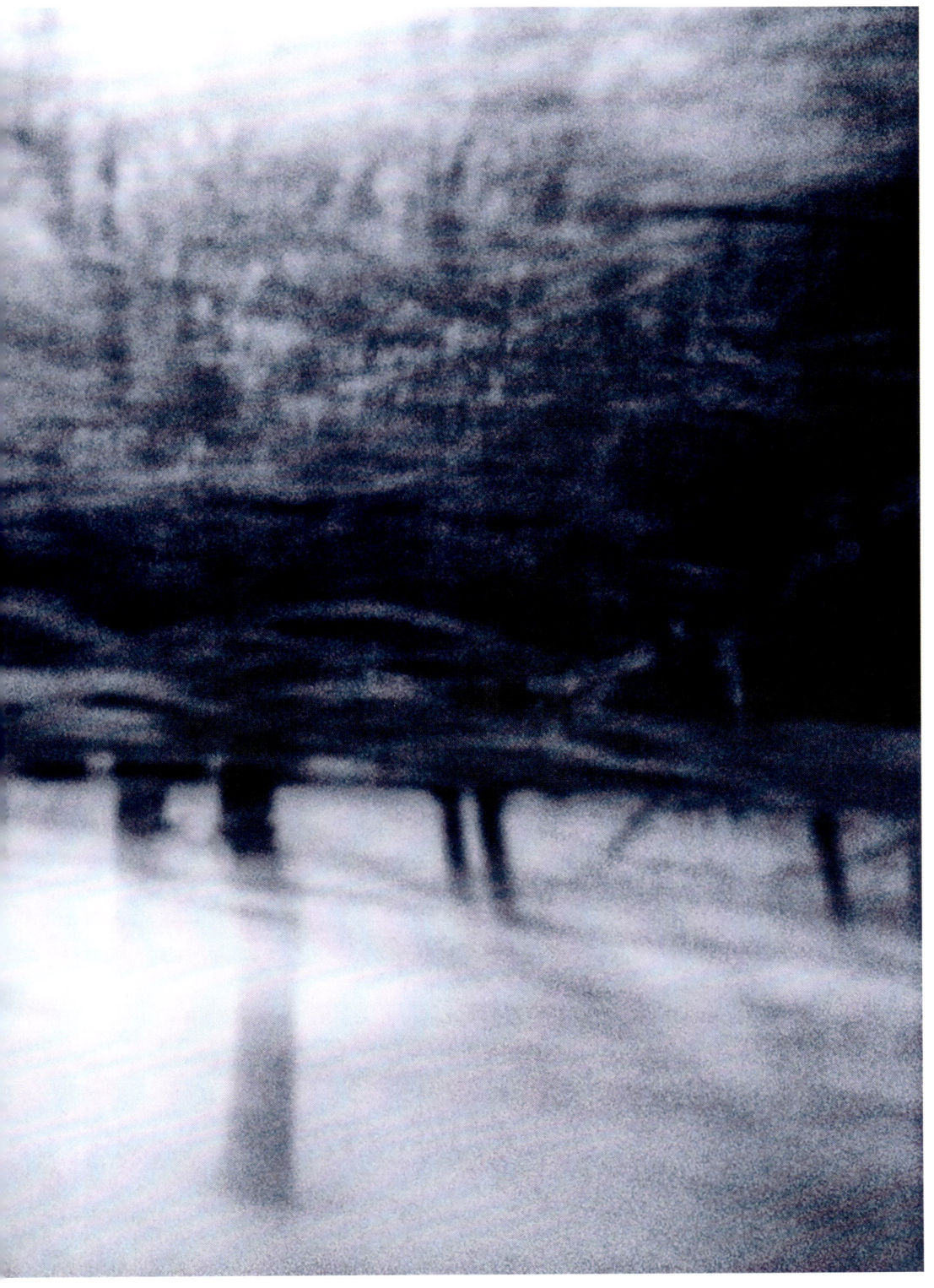

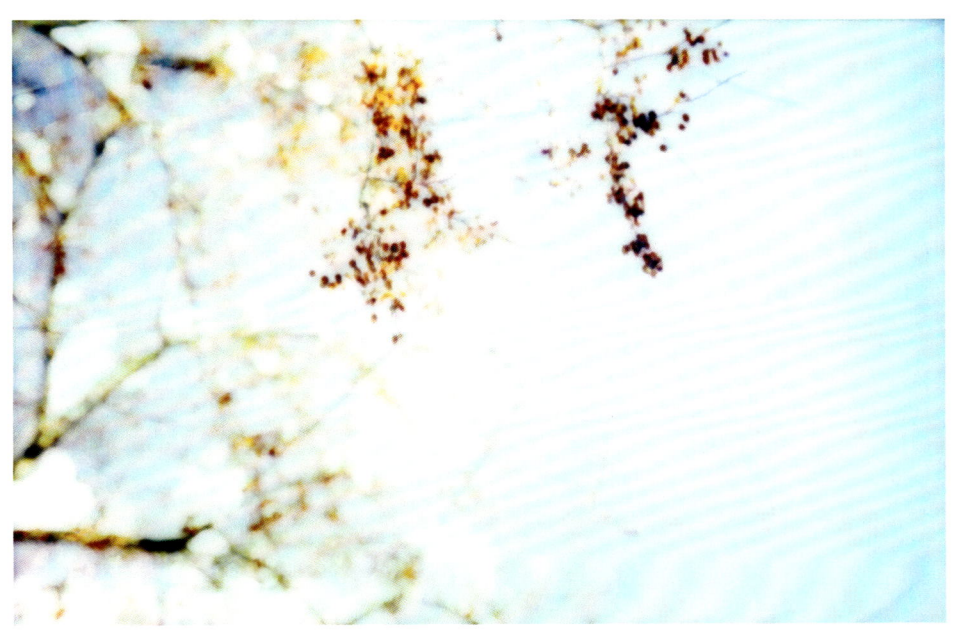

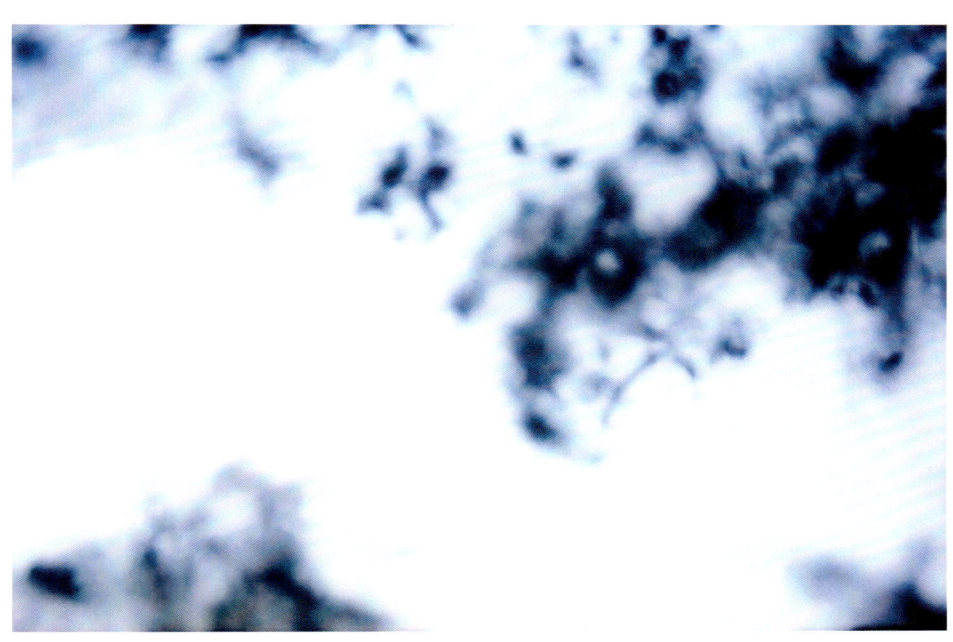

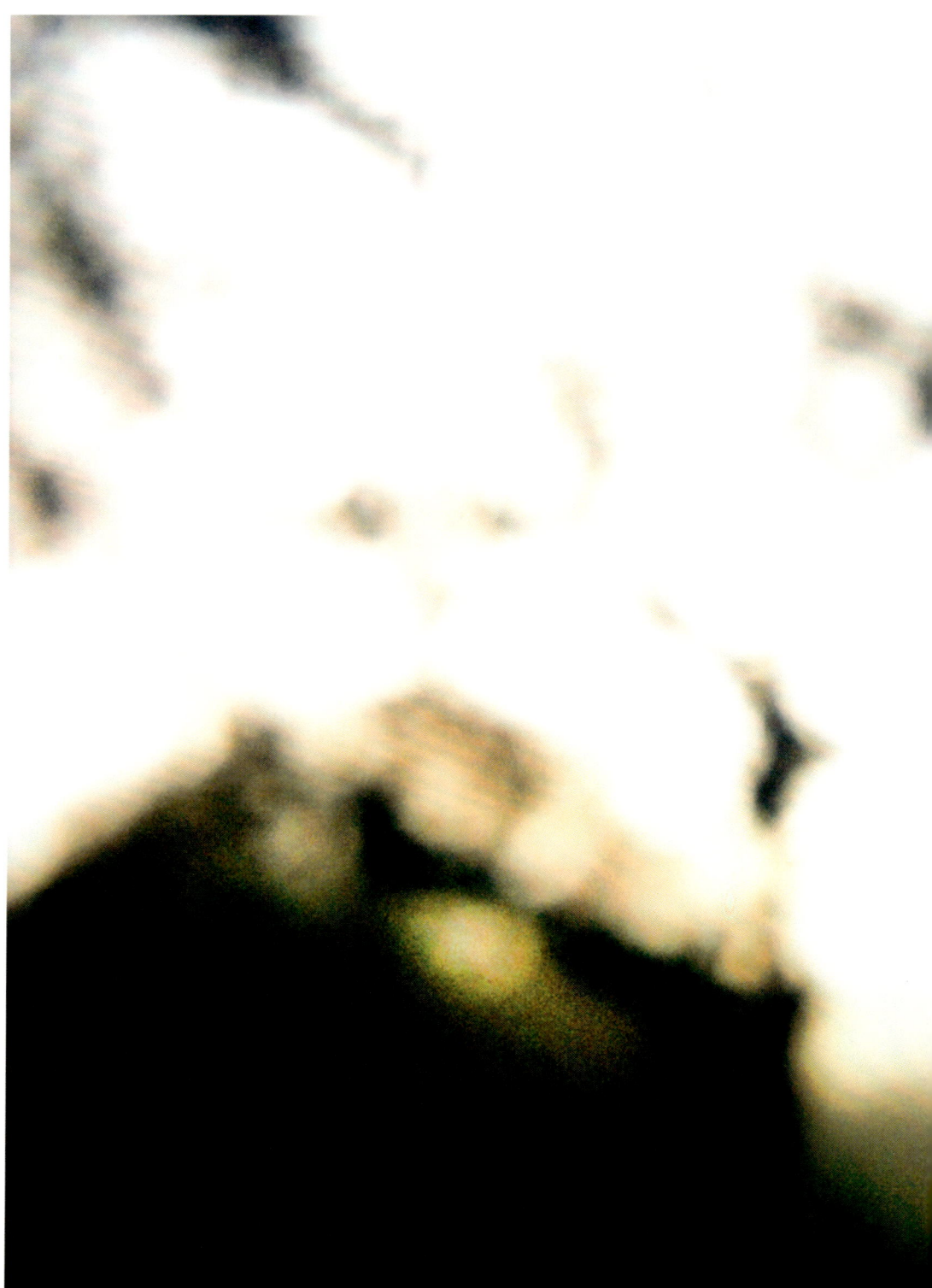

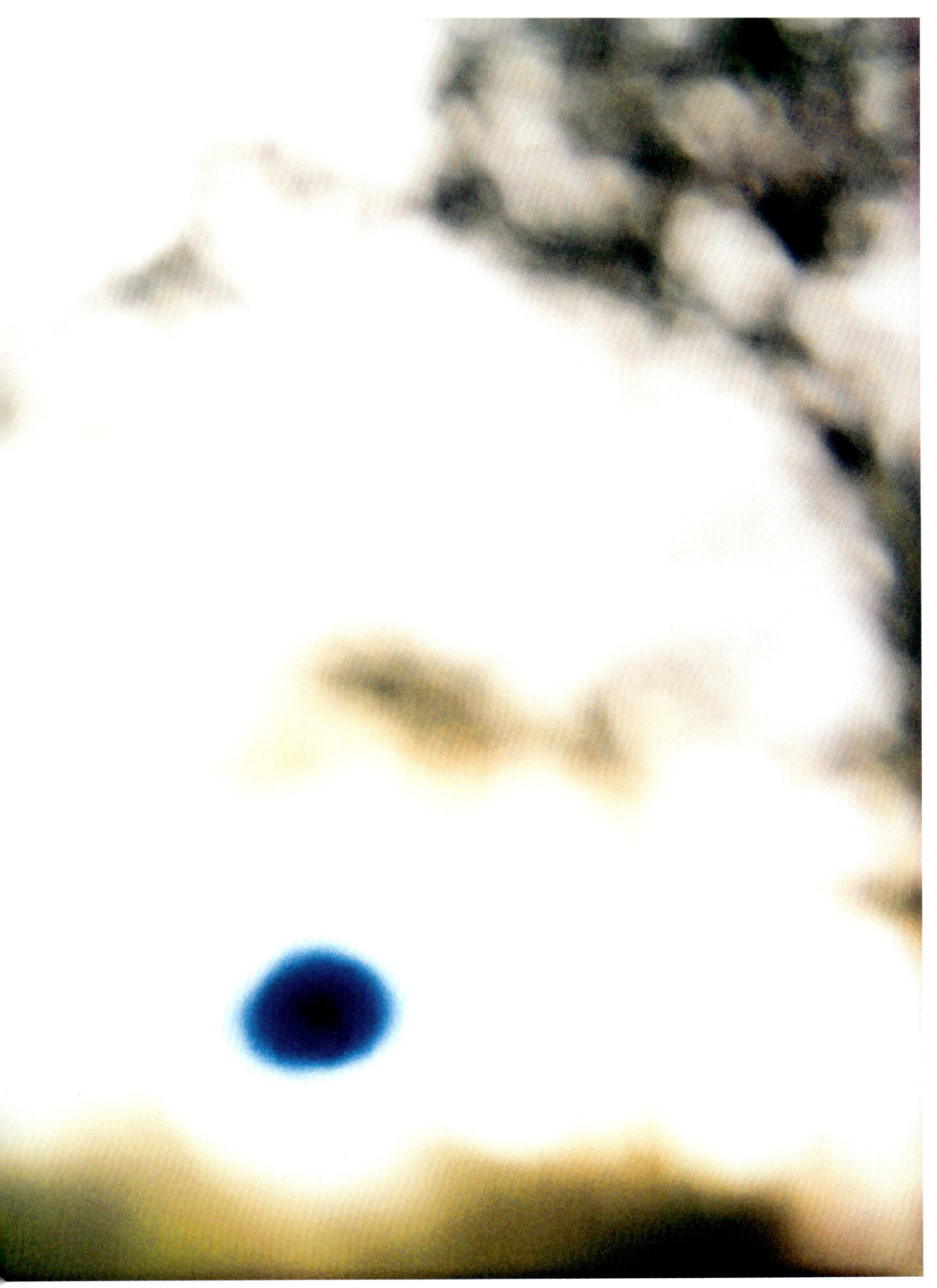

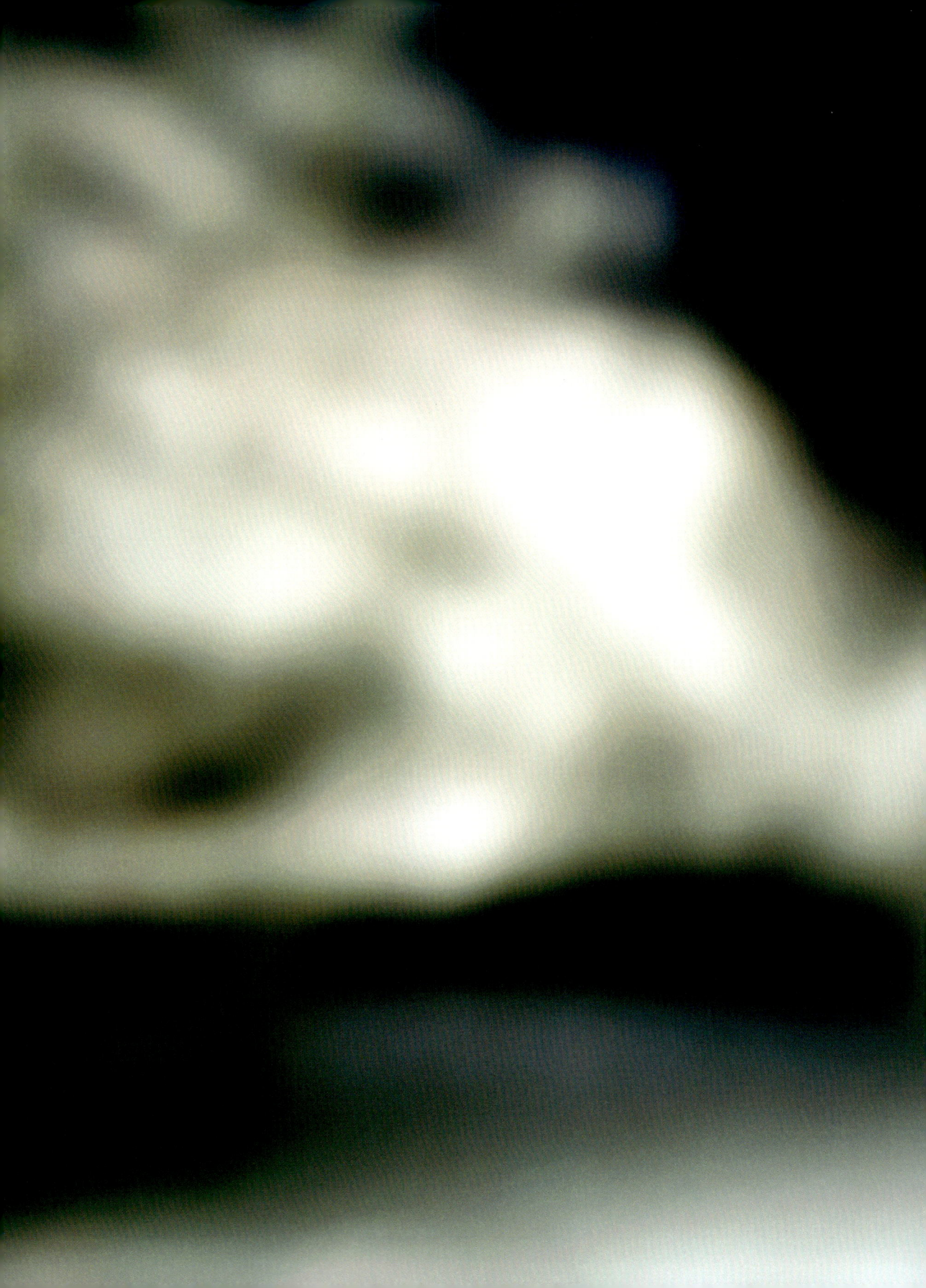

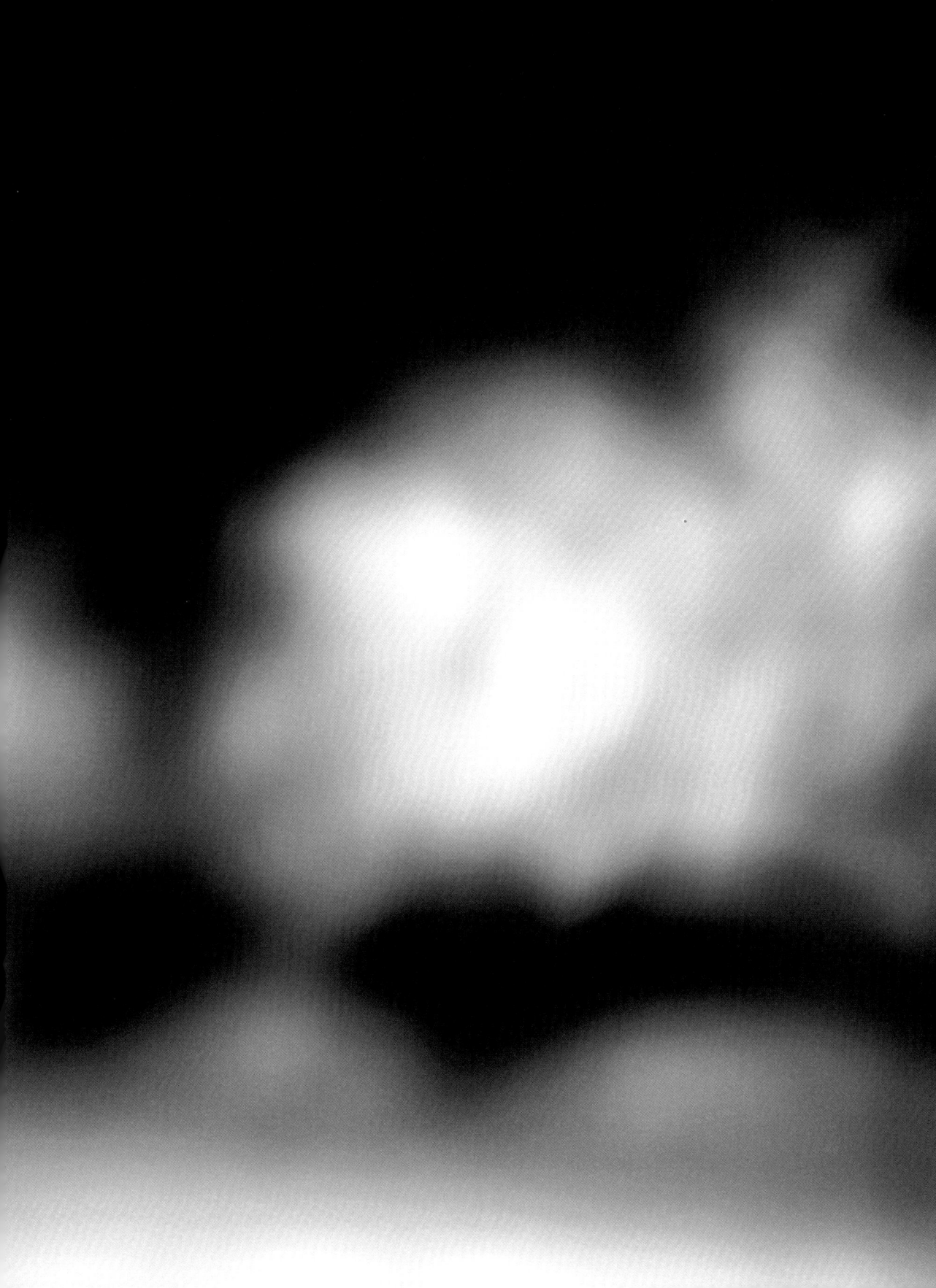

MY PROCESS

SUSAN WEISS

The isolated years 2020-2022 put many restrictions on my photography practice which was primarily documentary work until February 2020. January of that year I was photographing at the El Paso/Ciudad Juarez border to photograph the immigration crisis for a Washington D.C. based NGO. I remember brief discussions about some type of health crisis coming to America. Several weeks later I was suddenly in a position to rethink what I was doing and new ways to do it. I did not have access to a dark room but I still wanted to work with film. I also needed to have immediate gratification as proof of my process. I turned to an instant camera and instant film.

The images were made with a MINI InstantKon RF70 camera and the filters that accompany it. The film is Fuji Instax Wide with an ISO 800. Each film cartridge contains ten photographs. The prints were immediately scanned to preserve their color as the original photographs will degrade over time. They are stored in a black light proof box. There are over 500 photographs which were edited to the fifty presented in the book.

ACKNOWLEDGMENTS

The years of the pandemic, 2020-2022, were a very difficult time in Vermont, when strict rules were in place prohibiting socializing in groups and being with people that you did not live with. It also gave us time and space for inner reflection and thought, to find new ways of working and looking at life as it existed at that time. Priorities changed, daily habits changed, new social connections were made through the internet and social media connectivity with other people.

This work was produced during that period and at a time when I found solace and peace in nature and specifically an orchard. My daily ritual of photographing the seasonal changes gave my life structure and beauty. I was able to reflect on the passing of time and look forward to the future as expressed in the changing trees. This process gave me comfort and peace while there was chaos and sadness surrounding me.

I am deeply indebted to the following people who inspired and guided me with this work. Their knowledge and insights moved me forward to complete the project and create the book.

Harvey Stein
Tom Griggs
Stephen Schaub
Dean Darling

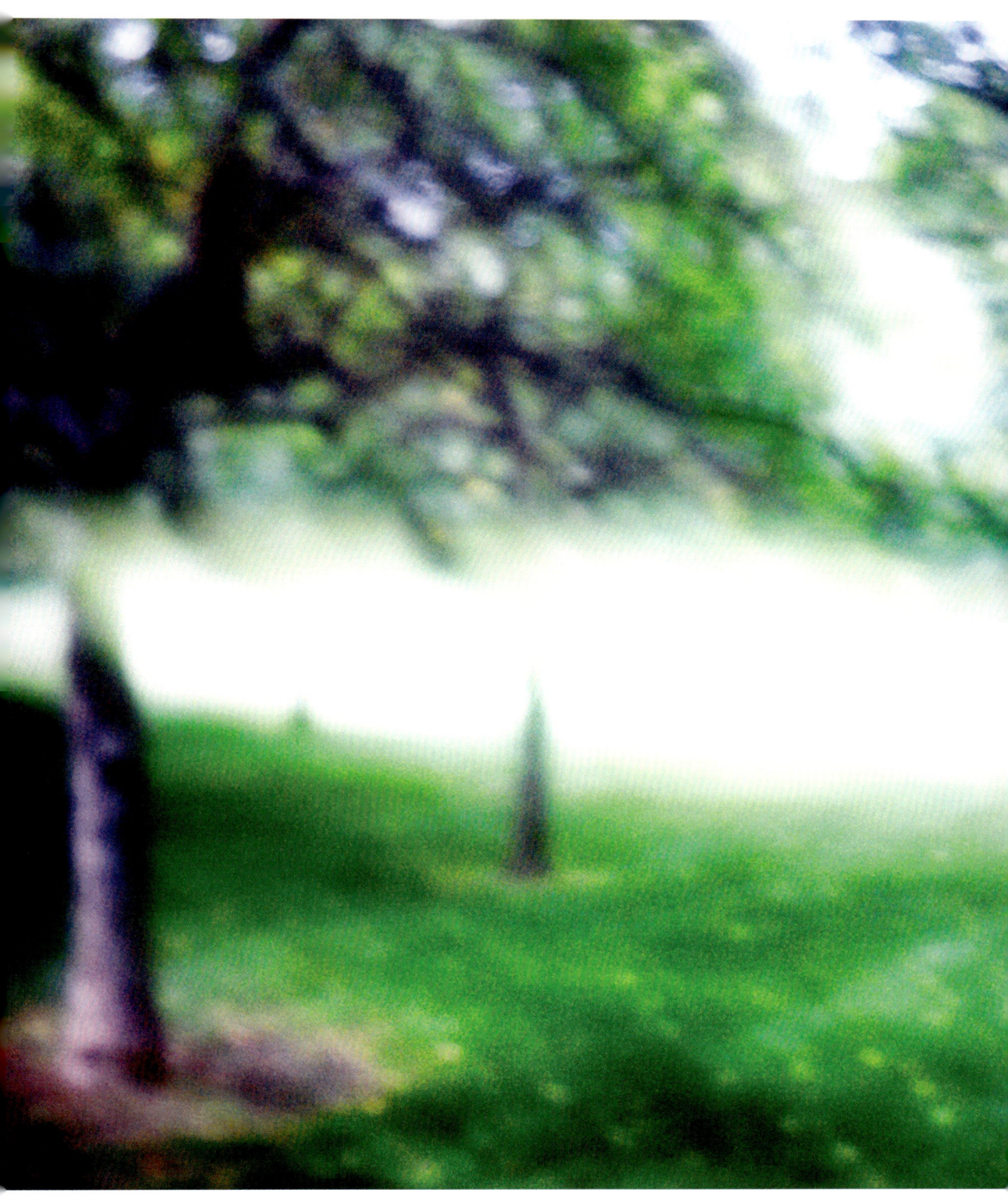

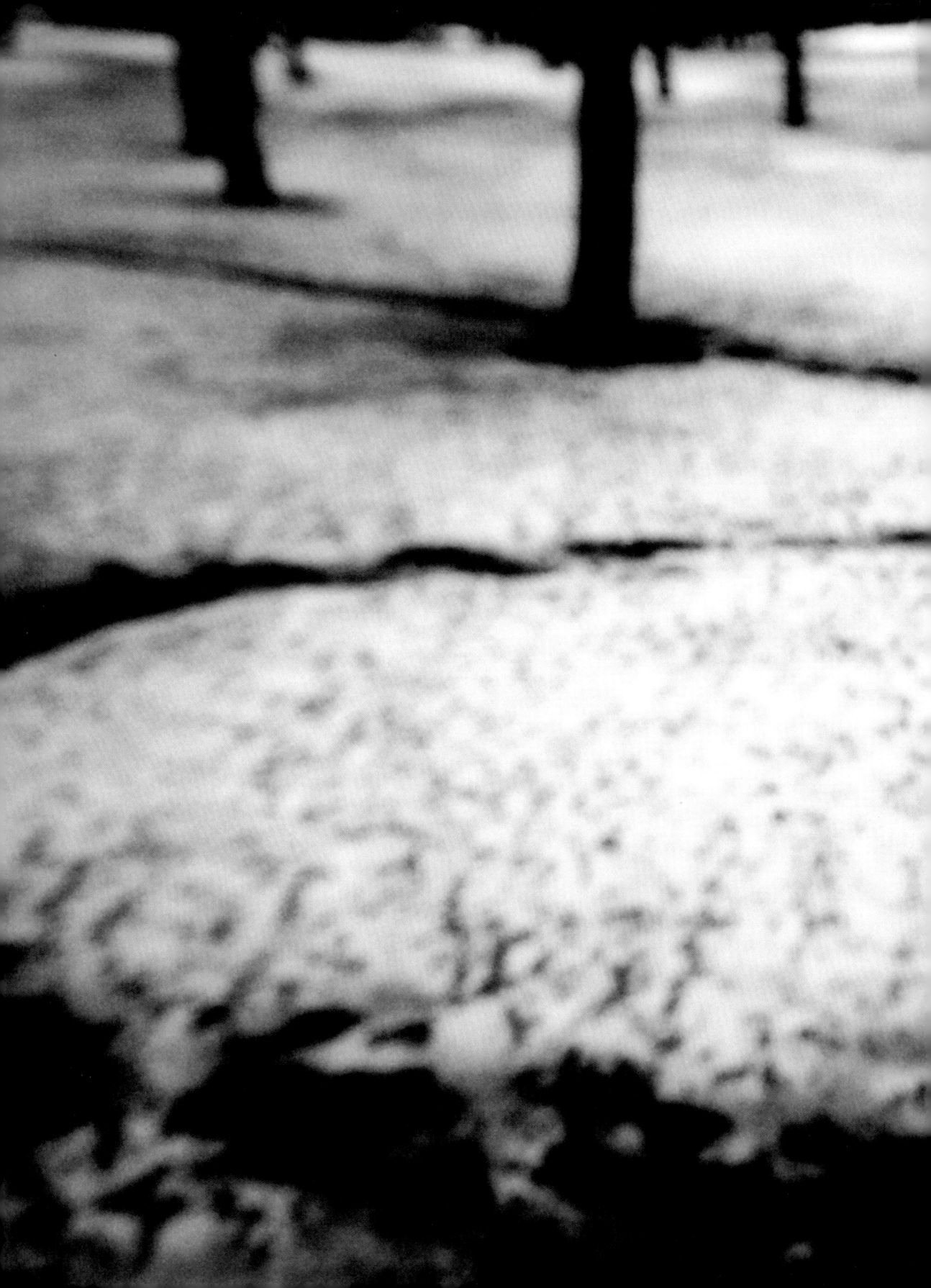

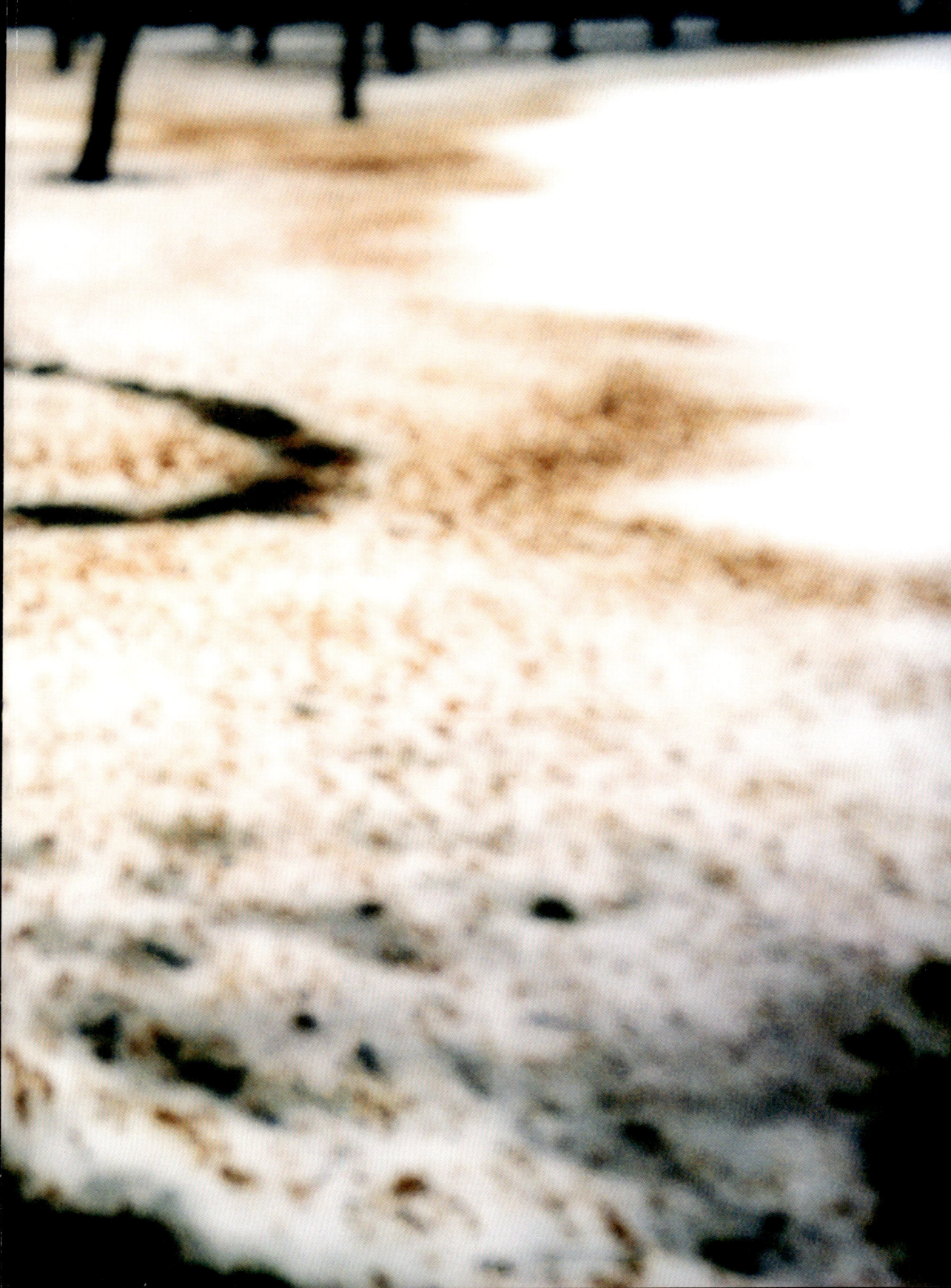

The Orchard BY SUSAN WEISS

BOOK DESIGN: DEDE CUMMINGS

PRINT/PRODUCTION SUPPORT: STEPHEN STINEHOUR

TYPESET IN ADOBE CASLON & HELVETICA NEUE

PHOTO SCANS BY STEPHEN SCHAUB

PAPER: 100# SILK TEXT, FSC CERTIFIED

COVER STOCK: 120# SPECKLETONE OATMEAL

BOUND BY SUPERIOR PACKAGING & FINISHING

BRAINTREE, MASSACHUSETTS

PRINTED BY PURITAN PRESS, HOLLIS, NEW HAMPSHIRE,
ON 30% POST-CONSUMER FIBER WITH STOCK SHEETS THAT
ARE FOREST STEWARDSHIP COUNCIL® (FSC®) CERTIFIED
THAT COME FROM MANAGED FORESTS THAT GUARANTEE
RESPONSIBLE ENVIRONMENTAL, SOCIAL, AND ECONOMIC
PRACTICES.